Keep Up
If You Can

To Dave & Alison!

Keep Up
If You Can

*Confessions of a
High School Teacher*

Dec 31/12

ENJOY! Bill
Sherk

*Bill
Sherk*

DUNDURN
TORONTO

Editor: Shannon Whibbs
Design: Jesse Hooper
Printer: Webcom

Library and Archives Canada Cataloguing in Publication

Sherk, Bill, 1942-
        Keep up if you can : confessions of a high school teacher / Bill Sherk.

Issued also in electronic formats.
ISBN 978-1-4597-0357-5

        1. Sherk, Bill, 1942-. 2. High school teachers--Ontario--Toronto--Biography. I. Title.

LA2325.S48A3 2012   373.110092   C2011-908027-3

1   2   3   4   5   16   15   14   13   12

We acknowledge the support of the **Canada Council for the Arts** and the **Ontario Arts Council** for our publishing program. We also acknowledge the financial support of the **Government of Canada** through the **Canada Book Fund** and **Livres Canada Books**, and the **Government of Ontario** through the **Ontario Book Publishing Tax Credit** and the **Ontario Media Development Corporation**.

Care has been taken to trace the ownership of copyright material used in this book. The author and the publisher welcome any information enabling them to rectify any references or credits in subsequent editions.

J. Kirk Howard, President

Printed and bound in Canada.
www.dundurn.com

Dundurn	Gazelle Book Services Limited	Dundurn
3 Church Street, Suite 500	White Cross Mills	2250 Military Road
Toronto, Ontario, Canada	High Town, Lancaster, England	Tonawanda, NY
M5E 1M2	LA1 4XS	U.S.A. 14150

To the love of my life, Lady Catherine,
to the memory of my mother, Edna Sherk,
and to my nearly seven thousand students,
this book is dedicated to you

Contents

The role of the editor is very much like that of the Wizard of Oz: "pay no attention to the man behind the curtain." But as one of Bill Sherk's former students, it's a great honour to briefly step out from behind the curtain and say a few words about a great teacher.

In grade nine, as a brand-new (and rather terrified) student at North Toronto Collegiate Institute, I took Bill's Canadian History course. Throughout my academic life, I had an appreciation for teachers who skewed their methods toward the unconventional and eccentric.

I immediately knew I was going to like Bill; his energy was palpable and he clearly had a passion for both the subject matter and for his responsibility in imparting the information to us. He was fair and reasonable and had a remarkable way of seemingly keeping the class under control without trying. I enjoyed having some light finally shed on these methods while editing this book. Sneaky, Mr. Sherk, sneaky!

On a Friday during the first month of the school year, Bill started the class by bringing out a portable stereo and introducing us to our very first Sherkout (an aerobic workout set to pop music, led by Bill himself — see page 121 for the full story). Bill leaped onto his desk and off we went. I couldn't stop laughing through the entire exercise — I was delighted. Not only was it a few minutes where we didn't have to take notes or learn, it was a fun opportunity to move around to music. And it was also liberating to see the entire class enjoying it.

The social universe of a high school is a complicated and messy collection of different cliques and groups warily orbiting one another. Everyone wants to be cool. No one wants to look like a loser. But during a Sherkout, we could drop the facade for a few minutes and all look ridiculous together, chanting, "Window! Door! Ceiling! Floor!"

In grade eleven, I enrolled in Bill's Ancient Civilizations class not because I was terribly fascinated by Ancient Rome, but more because I wanted to be in Bill's class again (and knew he would find a way to make me fascinated by Ancient Rome). It was another great year of Sherkouts and hand cramps from frantically copying down his endless notes. I was convinced at least half of the school's supplies budget went toward keeping Bill in chalk. He routinely filled all the blackboards in the room during a lecture, sometimes having to wipe off one or two in order to fit in all of his thoughts.

Which is why when it came time to name the book, I suggested *Keep Up If You Can*. Partially because it was what Bill said before he led his class in the very first Sherkout, and also because, as a teacher, that was precisely the challenge he issued to his students every year, day in and day out. Keep up if you can. And if you couldn't keep up, Bill was always there to lend a hand and get you back on track.

I am grateful to Bill for the experiences I had in his classroom. And I am thankful to North Toronto Collegiate for giving me opportunities to explore my interest in the written word. Starting with editing the weekly school newsletter (*The R.A.G.*) and the literary section of the school newspaper, those very early steps set me on a path to a career as a professional book editor. And when I came to work at Dundurn, I was reunited with Bill Sherk under an entirely different set of circumstances. I edited his most recent car book, *Old Car Detective, Favourite Stories, 1925 to 1965*, and suddenly the student was in charge of correcting the teacher's spelling and grammar! The second challenge was learning to call him "Bill" instead of "Mr. Sherk" (it's still hard!).

Bill and I had a wonderful time working together and when *Old Car Detective* was finished, he came to me with the idea for this teaching memoir. I was honoured to take the project under my wing and help him see it to fruition.

For a man to consistently out-energize a room of teenagers for over thirty years is an incredible feat, not to mention doing so with enthusiasm, passion, and genuine concern for his students. He has set the bar very high and current and future teachers should pay attention.

The role of the educator is ever-changing as different methods and obstacles arise. But the essence of the job is always the same: to teach and inspire and prepare students for future intellectual challenges. Which is why *Keep Up If You Can* is a worthwhile read for teachers and students alike. Even if you don't know Bill and were not one of his students, there is something for everyone in these heart-warming tales from the classroom.

Congratulations, Bill.
And thank you for all your years of service to us young 'uns.

Shannon Whibbs
North Toronto Collegiate Institute, Class of 1996
January 2012

Bill and I at the Dundurn office in late 2011. He presented me with a gift for a job well done on Old Car Detective. *A giant eraser to fix BIG mistakes. Ideal for an editor!*

With Special Thanks

Nearly seven thousand people made this book possible. To my students at Northern Secondary School and North Toronto Collegiate Institute, and the part-time students I taught at York University, you made it all worthwhile and you made this book a pleasure to write.

I remember three special teachers I had in high school at UTS. Ronald Ripley taught us the importance of memorizing poetry. Ken Prentice gave me the idea for giving ancient names to my ancient history students. And Andy Lockhart convinced me that teaching would be my life's calling.

Several of my fellow teachers deserve special mention. Nancy Baines of North Toronto Collegiate went through the school archives in search of suitable photographs. Dr. Surender Kumra persuaded me to help out at a school dance, thereby producing the photo you see on the front cover. My good friend, the late Dennis Pascoe, rounded up other teachers as passengers in my 1947 Mercury convertible for our lunch hour "Rock Around the Block." I also thank the librarians at Northern Secondary and North Toronto Collegiate for permitting me to look through school yearbooks to revive memories from my past.

Family and friends also deserve special mention. I thank my son Jeffrey and my daughter Juliana in sharing with me their enthusiasm for this book. Canadian author, historian, and good friend Scott Holland read extensive portions of the manuscript and offered valuable advice, especially with his encyclopedic knowledge of rock 'n' roll history. I thank Reverend Paul Rodey of the Leamington United Church for giving me the name of the Canadian poet (G.K. Chesterton) who wrote "The Donkey."

My former student, Shannon Whibbs, and now my editor at Dundurn, guided me with great skill and patience through the many details of editing and condensing thirty-one years of teaching to fit between the covers of this book. Shannon, I can't thank you enough! I also wish to thank the

Dundurn's senior designer, Courtney Horner, for creating the front cover of my book. I think it's hilarious!

And I extend a very special thank you to my special love, Lady Catherine, for her constant encouragement in helping me put down on paper the wonderful memories of my years in the classroom.

How Did I Do It?

You may be wondering how I managed to teach high school for over three decades. Well, when I landed my first teaching position in September 1966 at Northern Secondary School at 851 Mount Pleasant Road in Toronto, my wife, Joyce, and son, Jeffrey, and I lived on Castlewood Road and I walked to school every day. It took twenty-five minutes each way.

In March 1971, and soon after the birth of our daughter, Juliana, we moved to a larger house on Castle Knock Road, bringing me two blocks closer to school. The daily walk now took twenty minutes each way.

In October 1976, I was promoted to assistant head of history at North Toronto Collegiate, bringing me another two blocks closer to home. The daily walk now took fifteen minutes.

In addition to walking to school, both schools were three stories high and I climbed up and down the stairs in both schools for thirty-one years. I do believe that my years of walking and stair-climbing gave me the energy I needed to face 180 teenagers every day.

I still enjoy walking.

A Note to Teachers

Many of the teaching techniques I employed in my thirty-one years in the classroom were borrowed freely from other teachers and adapted to my particular teaching style. Other methods were uniquely my own as I tried to think of different ways to get my students interested in my subject, which happened to be history.

I sincerely hope you will be able to find ideas in this book that will be of help to you in the classroom.

Introduction

This book took forty-five years to write. I started teaching history for the Toronto Board of Education at Northern Secondary School in September 1966. I remained there for ten years (the same length of time Julius Caesar spent in Gaul), then taught history for another twenty-one years at North Toronto Collegiate, just two blocks west of Northern.

I could not have written this book before I retired in June 1997 at the age of fifty-five. It was my mother who was always after me to write it. I often told her of my many hilarious adventures in the classroom and she said, "Bill, you need to write these down and put them in a book. People will love reading it!"

Unfortunately, my mother did not live long enough to see this book become a reality. She passed away in October 2001 at age ninety-four, with me still promising that "someday" I would write the book she always wanted to read.

For the next several years, I kept myself busy writing newspaper stories and books about old cars owned and driven by auto enthusiasts all across Canada. Every so often, I would think about my mother and the book she wanted me to write.

Then fate stepped forward in a most unexpected way. Dundurn in Toronto asked me to write a book about old cars based on my syndicated weekly column, which, at the time of this writing, is carried in thirty-three Canadian newspapers with a circulation of over half a million readers. My new book about old cars was published in April 2011 with the title: *Old Car Detective Favourite Stories, 1925 to 1965*. It is now available in a bookstore near you. By an incredible coincidence, the editor who worked with me on that book is a former student of mine!

Shannon Whibbs, now managing editor at Dundurn, was in my history class at North Toronto Collegiate — twice! Canadian History in 1991 and again in 1994 for my Ancient Civilizations class. She also used to live just up the street from me on Castle Knock Road.

This was, I believe, a sign from my mother that I could no longer put off writing the book she always wanted to read. And so, here it is. It has been an exciting journey for me back into the past, back to the first day I stood, nervous and unsure of myself, in front of my first class. And now, forty-five years later, this book is finally written. I hope you enjoy reading it.

Bill Sherk
Leamington, Ontario
August 2011

My Frantic First Year at Northern Secondary School

1
On the Run to Fourteen Classrooms

A few days before I began my first year of teaching, I visited the school office at Northern Secondary and picked up my new timetable. I was going to be teaching two grade nine geography classes, two grade ten Canadian History classes, and two grade eleven Ancient and Medieval History classes. And I would be teaching these courses in fourteen different rooms all over the school.

At first, I felt very flattered that the school thought I was important enough to be teaching all over the building. Then an older teacher set me straight. I was at the bottom of the heap and did not qualify for a homeroom. I would be teaching in other teachers' classrooms when they had other duties.

The school was three stories high and it had an elevator, but I never used it except when showing an in-class movie on the first or third floor. The 16 mm Bell & Howell movie projector was kept in the history office on the second floor and whenever I needed it, I placed it on a trolley and weaved my way through the halls filled with students also heading to their next class, then took the elevator up or down if needed.

At age twenty-four, I took the stairs two steps at a time. I had only three minutes to get to my next class, and sometimes it was on the other side of the school, which covered an entire city block.

Each day's timetable followed its own unique sequence, and you had to keep a copy of it with you at all times. I taped mine inside the lid of my briefcase, but I also had to remember what day it was.

I rushed into class one day where the students were already seated and waiting for me. I opened my wallet and showed them a five-dollar bill with the face of Sir Wilfrid Laurier, our first French-Canadian prime minister. "Now, class, what did we learn yesterday about Sir Wilfrid Laurier?" I asked, hoping that someone would remember.

"Sir," said a student near the front, "we studied him last year in grade ten. This is your Ancient History class."

Without skipping a beat, I replied, "Well, I'm glad to hear you still remember Wilfrid Laurier from a year ago! Now let's turn our attention to ancient Egypt, where the pharaohs were building pyramids along the Nile ..."

By Friday of each week, I was running on empty, and prayed that my energy level would sustain me to the end of the day. It was also my heaviest teaching day, with seven classes to teach instead of the usual six. And my one and only spare was the very first period of the day. At precisely 9:40, I swung into action and taught four classes in a row all over the school, then made a mad dash for the basement where I had lunch in the teachers' section of the cafeteria.

After lunch, I climbed the stairs to the third floor, where I entered Room 307 for a grade nine geography class, then to Room 208 for a grade ten history class, then to Room 109 to teach my final class.

The bell rang at 3:20 p.m., signalling the end of the day and the end of the week.

Exhausted, I sat in my now-empty classroom till 3:25, then headed home on foot, lugging bundles of test papers and lesson plans in my brand-new Samsonite briefcase, later replaced by a gym bag because it was easier to sling over my shoulder, and thankful that my last three classes were in descending order of floors.

2

The Day the 7-Word Popped Up in Class

In my first year at Northern Secondary School, I taught a grade eleven Ancient History class consisting entirely of boys who were in the five-year Science and Technical program. Vic Priestley, age sixteen, sat at the back of the room and he also owned his own dump truck. He was in the landscaping business part-time on weekends, and although he wasn't at the top of my class, he wasn't at the bottom, either.

I phoned him one Saturday to do some work in our backyard. We needed a lot of earth brought over and he arrived with a good-sized load on his truck.

"I couldn't bring it all over at once, Mr. Sherk," he explained. "Kneel down at the back of my truck and I'll show you why."

I knelt down.

"Take a look at my rear tires." He had dual wheels at the back and the tires were almost touching one another because of the weight of the load.

"If I load up any more earth, the tires will rub against one another and I'll have a blowout. It's an old truck with old tires, but if I take good care of it, it will take good care of me. I'll have to make two trips to get you the earth you need, but I'll only charge you for one trip."

I thanked him and we unloaded the truck. Later, he delivered the rest of my order. Years later, Vic Priestley was in the demolition business and I often saw his sign all over the Greater Toronto area: PRIESTLEY DEMOLITION. I met him again at a gathering of old cars in Aurora. He owned a Model T truck with his business name on the door.

Mike McKernan was in the same classroom and sat in the row by the window. He greatly admired the late American President Kennedy, who had been assassinated just three years earlier. Mike could recite Kennedy's entire inaugural address from January 1961 and in the same Bostonian accent.

Eric Armstrong was a cheerful young man sitting in the first desk in the row by the door. He put up his hand one day and asked me if I knew any words that start with "F" and end in "U-C-K."

"That's a terrible question to ask me!" I replied in a stern voice. "I've a good mind to send you down to the office."

"I don't know why you're getting so upset, Mr. Sherk," he said. "The word I'm thinking of is 'firetruck.'"

I started to laugh, and discovered something that helped me survive the next thirty years in the classroom. If they can make you laugh, you can't really get too upset over something and you just carry on with the lesson while smiling over whatever happened.

And now I knew the answer to that question. I waited for it to pop up again.

It never did. I taught for thirty-one years and was only asked that question once. But I was ready with the right answer!

3

My First In-Class Movie Was a Disaster!

A movie arrived one day in the history office at Northern Secondary. Another teacher had already seen it and suggested I show it to my grade eleven Ancient History students. I didn't know how to operate the Bell & Howell 16 mm movie projector, but another teacher gave me a thirty-second crash course before I headed off to class.

I had the projector on a trolley and rushed down the main hall on the second floor, weaving around the throngs of students. I took the elevator to the first floor, then wheeled it around a corner and into the back of Room 110 on the north side of the school. The class was already there, waiting for me. I told them I was going to show them a movie. They responded with cheers and whistles!

"And," I said, "the title of the movie is ..."

Suddenly I panicked! I had forgotten to read the title on the film can and rushed to the back of the room. I quickly read the title, then rushed back to the front of the room and wrote the title on the board: *The Spirit of Rome.*

While they copied the title into their notebooks, I told them to write the numbers one to ten double-spaced down the left side of their page. The film was thirty minutes long and I told them they were to write down ten details from the movie while watching it, and I would collect their list at the end of the class.

I pulled down the screen mounted on two hooks at the front of the room and returned to the back of the room to thread the film through the projector based on the instructions I had received a few minutes earlier. The film followed a serpentine route around sprockets and levers and I nervously threaded it through until it looked good to go.

After instructing a student to close the curtains, plunging the room into darkness, I turned the switch to the "ON" position and the movie actually started! The fan made a whirring sound and the beam of light from projector to screen made the room look like a real movie theatre!

I positioned myself at the side of the room against the wall, halfway between the back and front, figuring that I would have a good vantage point from where I could watch the movie and at the same time keep an eye on the students, now visible in the glow from the screen.

The opening scene was shot from a hilltop overlooking a body of water. I can still hear the opening words:

> This is the Mediterranean ... Homer's wine-dark sea.
> Odysseus was storm-tossed here. Here rode the galleys.
> Above this inland sea loomed the promontories, the earth
> of Greece and Rome, their gods and laws. Go down into
> that water ...

The next scene took us underwater as the camera moved slowly among the ruins of a sunken Roman city. *Wow!* I thought to myself. *This is an incredible movie, far better than any I ever saw in high school. And I'm the one bringing this movie to my students. They must think I'm a great teacher!*

The narrator continued:

> This blue-green ambience, rippling into depths, stands
> well for an image of time. Here, in time's waters, recover
> the lost features: amphorae of dead gods and kings, ships
> and sunken cities, porches and columns of Rome.

Suddenly I heard a horrendous *crash* from the back of the room. The front reel had fallen off the projector and landed on the floor. But the projector was still running and the film was unwinding from the reel on the floor and grinding itself through the sprockets on the side of the projector! The image on the screen began jumping up and down and the narrator's voice sounded garbled, as if he were underwater amid the ruins.

Just as I took my first step toward the projector at the back of the room, the phone started ringing at the front of the room. I swung around and was about to rush to the phone, but stopped, thinking maybe I should shut the projector off first. I swung the other way toward the projector, then turned again toward the phone.

What if it's the principal calling? I thought. *But I don't want him to hear the noise the projector is making …*

Paralyzed by indecision, I swung back and forth several times, unable to make up my mind. Nothing in my full year of teacher training had prepared me for this emergency. The students stared at me, not quite believing what they were seeing.

Then: a miracle. A student at the back of the room reached over and shut off the projector. Another student answered the phone. It was a wrong number. And another student turned on the lights.

I ran to the projector and picked the reel up off the floor.

"I can help you, Sir," said another student behind me. I turned around and stepped aside as he explained that he set up movies for his teachers all the time and would be happy to help me. He threaded it properly through all the sprockets, then showed me the proper way to mount the reels on the arms of the projector.

"Sir, you have to push the reel on until you hear a *click*. That way, you know the reel is locked in place and it won't fall off."

I thanked him, then asked if it was ready to run again.

"It's ready," he said, then called to a student at the front to turn off the lights again. I turned on the projector and the movie began rolling again. It was in full colour and for the next thirty minutes, we were back in ancient Rome. It was an excellent movie and I showed it every year for the next thirty-one years. In my classroom, it fell on the floor only once.

I wonder if teachers these days have as many problems with DVD players?

4

The Day I Fell Asleep in Class

I fell asleep in class only once in my thirty-one years of teaching. It happened in my first year on the job. I had had a professor at the Ontario College of Education the previous year who told us that in our first year of teaching, there would be some nights when we wouldn't get any sleep at all because we would be up all night planning the lessons for the next day.

With this in mind, I did spend one whole night at home getting my lessons ready for the next day. They were masterpieces! I knew what I was going to say in every minute of every class. If it was possible to be overprepared, I was. My breakfast included a very strong cup of coffee.

I arrived at school and taught my morning classes with remarkable ease, considering I had been awake nonstop for the past twenty-eight hours. I then had a nice lunch in the basement cafeteria and headed off to teach my three afternoon classes.

That's when the lack of sleep caught up to me. I fought off the fatigue as best I could, and only yawned while writing something on the blackboard with my back to the class. Whenever I felt another yawn coming on, I would turn and write something else on the board, whether it was necessary or not. By the time I finished teaching my second last class, I was desperately in need of some sleep. I decided to show a movie in my last class to help me survive until 3:20 pm, the end of the school day. I hoisted the projector up on the trolley in the history office and headed to class, which thankfully was in the very next room. I parked the trolley at the back of the room, took the attendance, and wrote the title of the movie on the blackboard: *Turn of the Century*.

Then I walked to the back of the room. I was too tired to lift the projector off the trolley and place it on top of a desk, so I just turned it on where it was.

It was an excellent movie that highlighted the life and times in Canada from 1894 to 1914 with plenty of old photos, some early newsreels

— including the Great Fire of Toronto in 1904 — and lively commentary with period-perfect music. The students were captivated by the movie and watched it eagerly until the movie began moving sideways toward the corner of the room.

Just after it started, I sat in a desk beside the projector at the back of the room and rested my chin on my hands with my elbows on the desk. It was the first time in over thirty hours that I had shut my eyes. I nodded off and started leaning to one side. I leaned against the trolley and it started moving to one side, carrying the projector with it. That's when the movie started moving across the wall at the front of the room.

It reached the corner near the door, giving us a split-screen look, before I realized what was happening. A student tapped me on the shoulder and I woke up right away, straightened the trolley, mumbled something to the class about technical difficulties, and watched the rest of the movie with two elbows on the desk and both hands pulling up on my eyelids to keep me from falling asleep again.

5

Cartoon Maps on the Blackboard

When teaching a lesson, I made frequent use of the blackboard to illustrate what we were learning and to outline our topic in point form to make it easy to study from later on.

Because the events in history always took place somewhere, I found it handy to sketch various land masses quickly in order to show where places were in relation to one another, and to add arrows and other diagrams to further illustrate the lesson.

Speed was necessary and very important when drawing a map on the board, not only to keep the lesson moving along quickly, but also to reduce the amount of time I had my back to the class. Eyeball-to-eyeball contact was very important in maintaining an attentive class.

And so I developed a free-flowing style in sketching maps on the blackboard, and often told the students to sketch along with me, line by line. I could sketch these maps very quickly. To show just how fast I was, I told them I could sketch a map of the entire world, showing all the major land masses and bodies of water in less than five seconds.

Naturally, of course, they didn't believe me, and so I had to demonstrate this amazing skill right before their dazzled eyes. I picked a student with a watch that counted the seconds and told him or her to tell me when to begin.

"Mr. Sherk ... on your mark ... get set ... GO!"

I sketched the map of the world, then asked how long it took.

"Three and a half seconds!"

The map I sketched is on the next page looking exactly the way I sketched it on the blackboard every year for 31 years. Let's take a look at it ... MAP OF THE WHOLE WORLD.

At first, this map doesn't look anything like what you would find in an atlas, and yet, all I've done is straighten out all the coastlines. Believe it or not, this really is a map of the entire world. The concave curve at the top represents the Arctic Ocean. The three areas jutting down from it represent the three giant peninsulas that radiate out from the Arctic Ocean: North and South America, Europe and Africa, Asia, and Australia. And in between those land masses are the oceans. Antarctica is at the bottom.

The world in less than five seconds.

Now, you might ask, of what use is such a simplified map? Well, it illustrates the pattern of land masses around the world. Of more immediate value, by claiming I could sketch the entire world in less than five seconds, I got their attention.

Andy Lockhart, a very gifted teacher, was my history teacher when I was a student at UTS (the University of Toronto Schools). After I graduated with honours from the history program at the University of Toronto, I spent a year at the Ontario College of Education in preparation for a career in teaching. By an amazing coincidence, Andy Lockhart was now teaching there, and so the great teacher I had in high school was now the teacher teaching me how to teach!

One of the best pieces of advice he ever gave us was this: start each lesson in a way to deliberately capture the students' attention. My lightning-swift sketch map of the world always succeeded in doing just that.

The sketch maps that followed my sketch of the whole world in less than five seconds were more detailed, and they consisted of a combination of straight lines and curves that the students could draw line by line and curve by curve as I drew them on the blackboard.

My map of Australia provoked howls of protest from my students, who claimed I had drawn the map upside-down. "Why do you say it's upside-down?" I wanted to know.

"Because you've got north at the bottom. It's supposed to be at the top!"

"Why does it have to be at the top?" I would ask.

"Because north is always at the top of a map!" they would reply.

"And why is north almost always at the top?"

Dead silence as the question began to sink in.

Finally, a brave soul would venture a guess: "Because it looks more natural, being at the top."

"And why is that?" I would ask. "How and why did this practice begin of putting north at the top of our maps?"

Back and forth the speculation would go until we all finally agreed on one thing: north seems natural at the top of a map because civilization developed north of the equator, and because sailors followed the North Star.

"Now," I would say, "imagine you are flying nonstop from Canada to Australia. The airplane is heading more or less south and you have been invited by the captain to join him in the cockpit for the first view of Australia from the airplane. At six hundred miles an hour, it doesn't take long for the northern coastline of Australia to appear. And, if you sketched the entire continent from a very high-flying aircraft, north would be at the bottom and south would be at the top."

Another question from the class: "Sir, does this mean that all maps are right-side-up, no matter what direction is at the top?"

"Let's look in our atlas," I would say. And very quickly, the class would come up with the answer to that question. As soon as you put printing on a map, you have to be able to read it. And the printing — not the land mass — determines whether the map is upside-down or not.

I enjoyed teaching ancient Greek and Roman history because of the time we spent in the Mediterranean (Homer's "wine-dark sea"). I told them there are boats and ships in that body of water, but no trains, and so be careful how you pronounce the name of that body of water. It has

Eastern Canada.

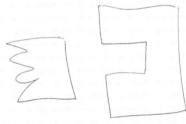

The British Isles.

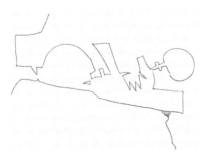

The Mediterranean.

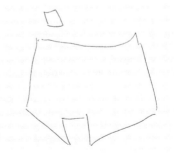

Australia (with the south at the top).

six syllables, not five, even though a lot of people will say "Meditrainean." Remember the syllable that many people skip over. The name of this body of water is the Med-i-*terr*-a-ne-an.

And why was it given this name? The name comes from Latin medi (middle) and terra (earth or world). The Romans conquered all the lands surrounding this body of water and called it the Mediterranean, meaning "the middle of the world."

6

Three Cheers for Jim McQueen

Cameron McQueen and I attended kindergarten together at John Ross Robertson Public School in the heart of North Toronto in the 1947–48 school year. We also attended grade one with Miss Longthorn and grade two with Miss Jones. Halfway through grade two (which was an accelerated class that would skip grade three), Cameron was promoted to grade four. And by the time the rest of us reached grade four, Cameron, a very bright student, was in grade five.

Fifteen years later, I became a teacher when I joined the staff of Northern Secondary School. I was pleasantly surprised to learn that Cameron McQueen's father, Jim McQueen, had served as principal of Northern from 1940 to 1954, when it was known as Northern Vocational School (the students called it "Norvoc"). His portrait still hangs in the front hall. The name had been changed to Northern Secondary School by the time I joined the staff in September 1966. I never had a chance to meet Mr. McQueen but I heard some admirable things about him from the older teachers on staff.

Jim McQueen always maintained that the most important people in the entire educational system were not the directors or administrators or even the teachers. The most important people were the students, and he insisted on teaching a class every day, even though, as principal, he didn't have to. He often said that he would get out of touch with what's going on in the classroom if he himself wasn't in there every day.

With over two thousand students attending the school, the principal's office at Northern was spacious and well furnished, and there were many demands on the Principal's time. Every so often, some directors from the Toronto Board headquarters at 155 College Street, along with some area superintendents, would meet with Jim McQueen in his office to discuss a variety of topics. And depending on what time of day the meeting was scheduled, it was not uncommon for Mr. McQueen to look at his watch during the meeting, then stand up and, with a smile on his face, announce: "Ladies and gentlemen, you will have to excuse me. I have a class to teach."

7

Keeping the Lesson Fast and Lively

In my first year of teaching, my classes were generally well-behaved, but there were days when they were restless and I could not seem to settle them down. Every five minutes or so, I was telling them to be quiet, and this was interfering with the delivery of the lesson.

In one grade eleven class, the student who sat at the front of the row by the window could see that the class was not entirely co-operating with me. His name was Bruce Andrews. Finally, he stood up, turned to the class, and said, "Listen here! Mr. Sherk is trying to teach us something and it's time for all of you to just SHUT UP and pay attention!"

To my great surprise, they shut right up and settled down. Bruce Andrews must have been a highly respected member of the student peer group because they obeyed him one hundred percent. Another student might try the same thing and be laughed at. But nobody laughed at Bruce.

But a teacher can't always count on having a student like Bruce Andrews in helping to maintain order. At one of the first staff meetings I attended at Northern Secondary, our vice-principal, Stewart Scott, gave us some valuable advice. He said the best way to guarantee a well-behaved class is to have a well-organized lesson.

I kept that in mind when planning my lessons. I didn't want the students to get bored or distracted, and so I kept coming up with a variety of techniques to keep them on track. One day, in the middle of a lesson, and with no advance warning, I said:

"EVERYONE STAND UP!"

They stood up.

"TURN AROUND AND FACE THE BACK OF THE ROOM!" I yelled.

They did.

"GET DOWN ON ONE KNEE!"

They did.

"NOW STAND UP AND FACE THE FRONT!"

They did.

"GET DOWN ON YOUR OTHER KNEE!"

They did.

"NOW STAND UP!"

They did.

"NOW SIT DOWN!"

As soon as they sat down, I continued with the lesson as if nothing had happened. I could always count on at least one student asking, "Mr. Sherk, what was that all about?"

I would smile and say in a loud voice, "EXERCISE!"

My techniques for crowd control began as soon as they were walking into the room. I would write the day's date high up on the blackboard over near the window, allowing room for the lesson to develop across the board.

As soon as they sat down, I would start barking orders like a football coach just before a big game, "Get those notebooks open! Copy down that date on the board and put it on a fresh sheet of paper!"

While I'm barking these orders, I'm clapping my hands together and walking up and down the aisles to see that everyone is getting down to business.

"Now get ready to copy down the title of today's lesson!"

I would go to the board and write in big capital letters *E-L-E-C-* …

"What is the rest of the word, and remember, we are studying Canadian politics!"

"I know, Sir! Electricity!" (There's always a joker in every class).

"You need another clue!" I would shout, and add two more letters *E-L-E-C-T-I* …

Then I shouted, "Just two more letters to go! You can raise your participation mark by getting this right!"

"Is 'election' the word you are looking for, Sir?" asked another student.

"Yes it is!" I shouted gleefully as I completed the word *E-L-E-C-T-I-O-N*.

"And the election we are talking about today took place seventy-six years ago! Who's a whiz at math? What year are we looking for? Oh, and by the way, the year we're in right now is 1987, in case you hadn't noticed."

Several hands shot into the air.

"Hey, we're really cooking! I'll bet the whole class has figured out the year, so right after I count to three, all of you will shout it out. ONE … TWO … THREE!" And the whole class shouted out, "NINETEEN ELEVEN!!!"

I finished writing the title on the board: *ELECTION OF 1911.*

"Now, who remembers the five-dollar bill I showed you a week ago? And whose face was on it?"

"Wilfrid Laurier!" a student proudly proclaimed.

"That's right! Mark his name down. He's the guy we've been studying all week!"

Just below the title I would write: *Wilfred Laurier.*

Then I said, "Ding-ding-ding-ding-ding-ding-ding …"

That always meant there was a spelling mistake somewhere.

"Sir," said the lad in the front row, "you spelled his first name wrong! It's not Wilfred. It's Wilfrid!"

"Thank you, George," I would say. "I'll remember you said that when I calculate the marks at the end of the term."

"Sir, you need to add something to the front of his name"

"And what is that?"

"He was *Sir* Wilfrid Laurier. The queen knighted him in 1897."

"And so she did!"

The lesson moved along with lightning rapidity as we consulted our textbook, talked about the election, drew some diagrams and headings on the board, and carried it right up to Laurier being turfed out and Borden coming in.

I summed it up this way: "The five-dollar bill got kicked out and the hundred-dollar bill came in!"

Keep the lesson moving by developing an outline on the board! Add some humour and physical exercise — and before you know it, the period is over!

8

She Was Only Fired Twice!

When I joined the staff of Northern Secondary in September 1966, a few staff members who began teaching at the school when it opened in 1930 were still there, including a commercial and business teacher named Annie O'Neill. My first year was her final year. She was quite a character. Short and stocky with gray hair and in her sixties, she drove to school in a low-slung Karmann Ghia sports car and reportedly had built a barn with her bare hands on a farm she owned outside the city. In June 1967, I attended her retirement party at our end-of-year staff luncheon in the school cafeteria in the basement.

Annie stood up and delivered a very short speech: "I've been teaching for forty years and I've only been fired twice, once for being too young and now for being too old. I'm leaving with mixed feelings but I'd hate to tell you what they're mixed with."

My Next Nine Years at Northern

9

The Man with His Face on Our Ten-Dollar Bill

Sir John A. Macdonald was Canada's first prime minister. He served from 1867 to 1873 and again from 1878 to 1891. Sir John A. came in handy whenever a student asked, "Sir, why do we have to study history?"

My reply: "Who can name the four Canadian provinces west of Ontario?"

The answer would come back: "Manitoba, Saskatchewan, Alberta, and British Columbia."

My next question: "And what is directly to the south of those provinces?"

"That's easy. Why, the United States, of course."

"And when all the good farmland got filled up in the United States, and this happened around 1890, where did American farmers turn to find new farmland?"

"Farther west?"

"No. The Rockies were in the way. Try another direction."

"North into Canada?"

"Yes, and many of them came here. But Sir John A. was worried about what might happen if the Canadian West was filled entirely with settlers from the United States. Why exactly was he worried about that?"

"Sir," replied one of my students, "maybe he was afraid that those Americans would want the Canadian West to become part of the United States?"

"Good point," I replied. "And had something like this ever happened before, somewhere else?"

Brief pause, then another question.

"Aside from Alaska, what is the biggest state in the United States?"

"Texas."

"Yes, and Texas at one time was part of Mexico. And at that time, American settlers were pushing west into lands that included Texas. Twenty thousand of them settled in Texas … and then decided they would like to be part of the United States. The result was a war that included the Battle of the Alamo, which the Mexicans won. But they lost the war and Texas became an independent republic in 1836 and joined the United States in 1845. Sir John A. did not want Canada to lose the West the way Mexico lost Texas, and that's why he worked so hard to push the Canadian Pacific Railway across western Canada to fill it with settlers — some, of course, from the U.S., but others from Europe and elsewhere. The last spike was hammered in at Craigellachie, British Columbia, on November 7, 1885, and those western lands are still part of Canada today. And that is one reason we study history, even though Napoleon said: 'The only thing we learn from history is that people learn nothing from history.' But why keep making the same mistakes over and over again? We owe a big debt of thanks to the man whose face is on our ten-dollar bill."

10

Engine Transplants Before Heart Transplants

Dr. Christian Barnard performed the world's first heart transplant in South Africa on Sunday, December 3, 1967, and the news flashed around the world. The recipient was a fifty-four-year-old-grocer named Louis Washkansky, who lived only a little over two weeks after the operation. But Dr. Barnard proved it could be done, and everyone knew more would follow.

The second heart transplant was performed by the same doctor on Tuesday, January 2, 1968. The recipient this time was Philip Blaiberg, a fifty-eight-year-old man who survived for nineteen months with the heart of a young man. The operation was a success; so much in fact that Bailburg felt much younger and enjoyed life much more.

We talked about it in class, especially how the doctor himself explained what he did to get the new heart started in the recipient's chest: "We gave it an electric shock and it started pumping right away. It was just like starting a car."

That quote got me thinking back to my history professor, Andy Lockhart at the Ontario College of Education, who had also been my teacher in high school at UTS (University of Toronto Schools). He told the student teachers that if they had any special interests or hobbies such as bird-watching, travelling, photography, or antique cars, they should look for ways to work those interests into their lessons to add extra sparkle to their teaching.

And so, by following that advice, I told my students that engine transplants had been performed ten years or more before the world's first heart transplant. They wanted to know more, and so I told them about my first car, a 1940 Mercury convertible that I had purchased in June 1959 for $150 with no engine. The previous owner had removed the engine so I could afford to buy the car. I was seventeen and in grade eleven. It was my high-school hot rod.

By the end of the summer, I had the car on the road with a '57 Chevrolet 283 V8 engine, a '38 Buick Roadmaster floor-shift transmission, and a '48 Ford rear end. I showed them the accompanying photo when I was trying to decide what kind of engine to install. They had lots of questions:

"Sir, how did you hook up the Chev V8 engine to the '40 Merc radiator? That rad had four openings, but the Chev only had two."

I had the answer. "With the help of a local auto mechanic, who actually had owned the same car two years earlier, we solved that problem by welding or brazing a metal cover over the two rad openings we did not need. A cheaper fix was to shave a block of wood into a taper, then tap it into each opening not needed. That was risky, because if the water pressure got high enough, the block of wood could pop out and you'd have water all over your engine. Next question …"

"Sir, what did you do for motor mounts? The Chev engine was not designed for a '40 Merc engine compartment."

This kind of talk was getting the class excited. Here they were in history class with a teacher who talked their language.

"My auto mechanic friend used the front mounts on the Chev engine and drilled holes in the front cross-member of the '40 Merc frame to mount them in. Today, you can buy ready-made conversion mounts, but back then, we had to make the parts we needed. Next question."

"Sir, what about your fan? Was there room for the Chev fan under the '40 Merc hood?"

"Yes, there was. We were lucky. Next question."

"Sir," asked another student, "did you have to modify the Merc frame in any way when putting in the Chev engine?"

"Yes. We had to cut a small notch in the passenger side of the front cross-member to make room for the fuel pump at the side of the Chev engine. Later on, I installed an electric fuel pump, which made the notch unnecessary. Next question."

"Was there enough room for the Chev starter motor?"

"Again, we were lucky because it was on the passenger side of the engine. But a friend of mine in high school dropped a Buick V8 into a '40 Ford coupe around 1962 and the starter motor was on the driver's side and interfered with the steering box."

"What did he do?"

"He took it off and threw it away."

"Then how did he start his car?"

"He lived on a hill and let the car roll down a ways, then popped the clutch and away he went. Next question …"

And so it went. We only spent about five minutes on all of this, but it was a good change of pace. Then back to our course of study.

Here I am at seventeen in 1959, staring into the empty engine compartment of my 1940 Mercury convertible and wondering how I can install a more modern engine.

11

Her Dog Had Fleas

Many of the students in my Current Events evening school classes at Northern Secondary were seniors living on a pension. They enjoyed the course because it gave them an opportunity to go out and socialize with other people and learn something about what was going on in the world at the same time.

After we discussed various items in the news, we would take a fifteen-minute break for coffee, or to just stretch our legs. That's when I got to talk to my students on an individual basis, and in doing so, I learned a number of fascinating things.

A lady named Margaret Scott told me one night that times were tough and she could not afford to buy a flea collar for her dog. But she figured out a way to help Fido stop scratching. She lived near the Riverdale Zoo in downtown Toronto and walked her dog over there every day and had him sit in front of the monkey cage. The monkeys reached out, picked the fleas off his body, and ate them. Her dog enjoyed the free massage.

12

History Teacher Pumps Gas at Local Station

My brother-in-law, Nelson Gray, lived with us in Toronto during the 1968–69 school year in order to return to school and complete his education. He also took on a part-time job pumping gas at Harold Lehman's Esso station at Bayview and Broadway, the same station where I had worked a few years earlier while attending university.

When the Christmas holidays rolled around, Nelson returned to Leamington to spend the holidays with the rest of his family. I volunteered to fill in for him at the gas station during his time away to make sure his job would be waiting for him when he returned to school in January.

During my two weeks at the station, several students of mine pulled in for gas and were surprised to discover that their history teacher was filling their tank. They seemed to enjoy the role reversal and I got a kick out of it, too. They made sure I cleaned their windshield and looked under the hood to check their oil, rad, and battery. This was all during December, on some of the coldest nights of the year. And I always gave them service with a smile.

I even suggested checking the air in all their tires, and several of them pulled over to the side and parked in front of the air hose. One student actually gave me a twenty-five-cent tip as a reward for my excellent service, and maybe also hoping for a better mark in history!

I was glad I had already worked there part-time six years earlier because I knew exactly what to do. On my first night on the job in January 1962, I had no idea what I was doing, and had to learn the ropes very fast.

The first car I served was a 1954 Ford sedan, and the driver wanted "two bucks of the cheap stuff." I lifted the nozzle off the pump and pulled the rear licence plate down to expose the gas cap. My mother and dad had owned a pair of 1954 Fords, and so I knew exactly where the nozzle should go in.

But this man's cap was frozen shut and wouldn't budge. Finally, I held the nozzle between my legs and had to use both hands to get the cap unstuck. Then I shoved the nozzle in and squeezed the handle. Nothing happened.

Then I noticed I had forgotten to turn the pump back to zero to erase the previous sale. I let go of the nozzle to flick the switch on the side of the pump, and that's when the nozzle popped out of the filler neck and fell into the snow. In my haste to put it back in before anyone saw it on the ground, I tripped over the hose and landed in the snow on my hands and knees. The driver began adjusting his rear-view mirror to see what was going on at the back of his car, and the car behind me backed up and went to another pump.

I finally got the gas flowing into his tank, then couldn't remember how much he asked for. "Did you want it filled up?" I yelled. I wasn't going to leave the hose to walk to his door. Unfortunately, his window was rolled up and his heater was on full blast. He couldn't hear me. He finally heard me on the third yell and held up two fingers.

In my first hour on the job, I had to find gas filler caps in every place imaginable. On a '56 Chevy, you had to turn a section of the left taillight to get at it. On a '57 Chev, it was hidden behind the left tailfin. On a 1958 Chev, the gas-cap flap was cleverly concealed in a section of the body between the trunk lid and rear bumper. The 1959 Chevy had it behind the rear licence plate, just like the 1954 Ford. I wondered why the designers at Chevrolet couldn't decide where to put it.

I worked four hours on my first night, from six to ten, and those four hours were a blur as the customers bombarded me with orders: "Three dollars of hi-test and make it snappy."

"I think you better check my tires."

"Don't use that oily rag on my windshield!"

"I need the key to the washroom."

"Could you check my antifreeze?"

"One of my headlights is burned out."

"I can't get my trunk open; the lock's frozen."

My worst mistake of the evening was putting five bucks' worth of gas into a car, then having the customer insist he had only asked for two. I had to use a rubber hose and gas can to siphon out three bucks. And that's when I got a mouthful of gasoline.

When my shift ended at ten, I thought I was going to be fired. My boss, Harold Lehman, pointed an angry finger at me and said, "You march yourself into the office and tell Jimmy to give you all the extra hours he can because you need the practice real bad!"

13

Effective Writing for Nineteen years

On Saturday mornings for nineteen years, from 1969 to 1988, I taught a non-credit Effective Writing course at the Glendon Campus of York University through the Centre for Continuing Education. Another course, Creative Writing, dealt with fiction-writing and my course dealt with non-fiction.

About fifteen people signed up for each class, which ran for ten weeks. Some were university students, others were business people, some were retired, and all had one thing in common: they wanted to improve their command of the written word.

I acquainted them with the Three P's: Prepare, Produce, and Polish. In the "prepare" stage, you list in point form everything you want to mention in what you are going to write, then you arrange these points in a logical sequence. In the "produce" stage, you convert all your point-form items into sentences and paragraphs. In the "polish" stage, you read it over very carefully to make corrections and improvements. Many of the students admitted that they had never made use of the first or third step.

I also drew my students' attention to a slim little paperback called *The Elements of Style* by William Strunk and with a foreword by E.B. White of *Charlotte's Web* fame.

Strunk was a professor at Cornell University in upstate New York many years ago and gave lectures on communication, especially on writing. His three favourite words were: "Omit needless words!" He was so fond of saying this, and he believed so passionately in the importance of it, that he usually said it three times in a row:

"Omit needless words! Omit needless words! Omit needless words!"

We tackled assignments in the writing course with Strunk's words in mind, and this was probably the single most important benefit of the course. With each passing year, I helped the students develop a more concise and, therefore, more effective writing style. At some point in those nineteen years of teaching that course, I came up with the single sentence that I urged students to remember even if they forgot everything else we talked about. This single sentence contains the magic recipe for effective writing, and here it is (drum roll, please!): *Choose the right words and put them in the right order.*

And how do we find the right words? By listening to the natural rhythm of the English language.

E.B. White started his writing career as a cub reporter at a Seattle newspaper. On one of his first assignments, he was sent to the morgue to get the story of a woman who had been murdered. Just as White arrived, another man was brought in to see if the murdered woman was his wife. When the sheet was pulled back, he looked down at her face and cried, "My God! It's her!"

White included that quote in his write-up for the paper and passed his story along to his editor, who was a real stickler for grammar (and usage be damned). White's story was published the next day with one change. The quote now read: "My God! It's she!"

White did not want to work for an editor whose obsession with grammar blinded him to the natural rhythm of the English language, and to the point where he would go so far as to alter a direct quote. White resigned and moved on.

One of my favourite writing assignments for my classes at York was an exercise called "Why I'm Crazy About …" I asked the students to write about something they were really crazy about — travel, cooking, gardening, music, sports, whatever. Then I said, "You have to compose a paragraph describing what you are crazy about. You can use only three sentences. The first sentence introduces the topic. The second sentence gives more detail. And the third sentence wraps it up."

I then gave them a few minutes at their desks to compose their paragraph. When they finished, I sat the class in a large semi-circle and each student took a turn reading what they had written to the class. I copied each paragraph down on the blackboard and we discussed how effective it was and if it could be improved.

The last person to read aloud was a woman around her mid-forties with a pleasant voice and a nice smile. I will never forget what she wrote:

Why I'm Crazy About My Children

I must be crazy! Labour pains ... growing pains ... leaving pains ... maybe I'm not so crazy after all.

In just seventeen words, she described as a mother the journey from birth to adulthood for her children, and decided it was all worthwhile. Everyone in the class agreed she had written a masterpiece.

14

A Turkey Almost Landed on the Moon

For those of us who are old enough to remember, we witnessed one of the most outstanding historical dates of all time: July 20, 1969. That's the day Neil Armstrong set foot on the moon — the first man from Earth to do so. When he reached the ground, he uttered those immortal words: "That's one small step for man, one giant leap for mankind."

When his spacecraft touched down on the lunar surface, he radioed back to Earth the words everyone was hoping to hear: "Tranquillity Base. The *Eagle* has landed!"

All this happened during the summer, when I had no students to teach. When we returned to class in September, we talked about this historic event in class, and I mentioned something about the moon landing that my students probably had not yet heard:

"The spacecraft that landed on the moon was, of course, named after the national bird of the United States — the bald eagle. But not everyone over two hundred years ago was happy with that choice. Benjamin Franklin recommended that the turkey gobbler be adopted as the national bird because of its central role in Thanksgiving celebrations every year. Well, as we know, old Ben was outvoted on that one, and maybe it's just as well. If he had had his way, those words coming to us from the moon would have been a little different: 'Tranquillity Base. The *Turkey* has landed!'"

15

"Flushed With Pride"

Robert Correll was a student in my grade ten Canadian history class in the 1969–70 school year. One day he brought to class a book review from a magazine because he thought I would enjoy seeing it.

The book was *Flushed With Pride* by Wallace Reyburn and it told the life story of a sanitation engineer in England by the name of Thomas Crapper. I had never encountered that particular family name before and wondered if the book was pulling our leg. None of my more than six thousand students were Crappers, but when I checked the Toronto telephone directory, I found listings for twelve Crappers.

It seems that Thomas Crapper had quite a career. He installed all the royal flush toilets at Sandringham for the benefit of King Edward VII and Queen Alexandra. In one bathroom, there were two flush toilets side by side and a crown up on the wall behind each one.

Crapper's Automatic Flush was a toilet that automatically flushed as soon as you put the lid down. He also installed toilets in prisons in such a way that the pipes leading to the toilet were concealed. Apparently some inmates had been in the habit of breaking off exposed pipes and bashing the guards over the head.

And now for a story about toilets that might be apocryphal (that word sent my students running to the nearest dictionary). Many years ago, someone told me that all the flush toilets at Westminster Abbey played a very important role in the preparations for the coronation of Queen Elizabeth II in June 1953. The planners for the event left no stone unturned and, as it turned out, no toilet unflushed in making sure that everything went smoothly and with great dignity.

That's when one of the planners had a horrible thought. Many members of the House of Lords were quite elderly, and suppose one or more of them had to visit the "loo" in the middle of the ceremony. Wouldn't it be awful if, just at the instant when the crown was being placed on Quen Elizabeth II's head, the assembled crowd and people around the world watching on television could hear a toilet being flushed?

To determine whether or not this might happen, a crew was assembled and instructed to go to every washroom in Westminster Abbey and, on a pre-arranged signal, flush every toilet simultaneously while other members of the team, especially those with excellent hearing, stood on the exact spot where the crown would be placed on the Queen's head.

No one heard a single flush.

16

"Cooks, Gluttons, and Gourmets"

Jay Wright was a student at Northern Secondary in my grade eleven Ancient History course. He brought to school one day a book of cooking and eating habits down through the ages entitled *Cooks, Gluttons, and Gourmets*.

I read portions of this book to my students, and the most fascinating part for them was the chapter on ancient Rome. They were both intrigued and revolted at learning that wealthy Roman villas in Caesar's time often had a room adjacent to the banquet hall where dinner guests could go in order to throw up their meal so that they could go back to the table and start eating again. One wealthy Roman even had a slave whose sole responsibility was to tickle the back of his master's throat with a feather to make him puke.

The room was called a "vomitorium." A couple of my students volunteered to re-create the sounds that surely must have emanated from such a room. With the use of a tape recorder carefully lowered into a toilet bowl at home, they made retching sounds and then flushed the toilet. They brought the recording to school the next day and played it for the benefit of the class just before lunch.

17

Julius Caesar Was in My Class! Cleopatra, Too!

I taught the grade eleven Ancient and Medieval History course in every one of my thirty-one years in the classroom.

Early in my career, I decided to give my students the opportunity to have an ancient or medieval name for the duration of the school year. I got this idea from my high school Latin teacher at UTS, Mr. Ken Prentice. Three students in the class all had the same last name: Wright. We were all addressed by our last names in class, and so for the Wright fellows, he named them Primus, Secundus, and Tertius.

I handed out a sheet to my grade eleven students on opening day called "Putting Flesh and Blood on the Bare Bones of History." I gave each student until the end of September to select an ancient or medieval name on a first-come, first-serve basis. They could look through our textbook or go to the library in search of the name they wanted. As soon as they made their selection, I marked it down beside their regular name on my seating plan.

At the end of September, I made out a new seating plan. Now everyone in the class was sitting in the order in which they lived, with the most ancient names over by the window and less ancient ones near the door.

The row by the window tended to have names from Ancient Egypt and throughout the Middle East, including Abraham, Hammurabi, Nebuchadnezzar, Ramses III, Nefertiti, and Moses.

The second row in from the window usually had names from ancient Greece, whether of real people or of the gods and goddesses on Mount Olympus. Perennial favourites included Homer, Herodotus, Alcibiades, Thucydides, Aeschylus, Pericles, Euripides, Darius and Xerxes (from Persia), and Alexander the Great (and his horse Bucephalus) from Macedonia. Ulysses was often chosen, as well as Aphrodite, Hera, Athena, Zeus, and Cassandra. And let's not forget Aegeus and his son Theseus.

The ancient Romans usually filled the centre row with Tarquin the Proud, Cincinnatus, Pompey, Crassus, Julius Caesar (immortalized by the Canadian comedy team of Wayne and Shuster in their classic skit: "Rinse the Blood Off My Toga"), Marc Antony, Hannibal from Carthage, Lepidus, Spartacus, Augustus, Hadrian, Constantine, Nero, Claudius, Boadicea, Vercingetorix from Gaul, and hundreds more, including Cicero, the Gracchi brothers, and Romulus Augustulus.

In the fourth row from the window, we usually ended up with names from the Dark Ages and Middle Ages, including Attila ("I will reap the windy swathes of diamond night and hoard the stars in pits against the winter"), Geoffrey Chaucer, the Venerable Bede, St. Benedict, St. Francis of Assisi, Pope Urban II, Richard the Lion Heart, Wat Tyler, Joan of Arc, Mohammed, and many others.

Finally, the row by the door represented the Renaissance up to around the year 1600. In this row from year to year could be found such notables as Michelangelo (who painted with a brush instead of a roller), Leonardo da Vinci (who wrote backwards), Prince Henry the Navigator, Vasco da Gama, Vasco Nunez de Balboa, Christopher Columbus, Amerigo Vespucci, Martin Waldseemüller, John Cabot, Johann Gutenbuerg, William Caxton, Martin Luther, Henry the Eighth and all his wives, Elizabeth (the "Virgin Queen"), Sir Francis Drake, the Bard of Avon (a.k.a. William Shakespeare), Nicholaus Copernicus, and Pope Gregory XIII, who gave us the Gregorian Calendar, which we use today.

Tell us all about yourself!

Whenever we reached a certain character from the past whose name lived on in my class, that person went to the front of the room and told us all about themselves. Sometimes several of them went to the front to put on a performance.

I remember one year when a young lad decided to be Homer (the Greek poet who penned *The Iliad* and *The Odyssey*). He ended up in the second row populated entirely by girls who had taken the names of Greek goddesses. When their turn at the front rolled around, Homer went out into the hall, then had a friend announce his arrival with the theme song from *The Tonight Show* playing on a boom box followed by: "And now, her-r-r-r-r-e's HOMER!"

Homer (*a la* Johnny Carson) came out, sat at the front desk, and interviewed each one of the Greek goddesses as if they were Hollywood starlets. The class loved it!

And now, a prehistoric name!

A girl in my class one year wanted to be called "A-hem" (the sound of one clearing one's throat). I asked her who this was in the past. She says it could have been the name of the person in prehistoric times who first learned how to make fire. That topic was part of the introduction to our course and "A-hem" she was! I had to clear my throat every time I spoke to her in class.

What to call the teacher?

After all the names were selected and I moved everyone around to sit in chronological order, the inevitable question arose: "Mr. Sherk, what ancient name will you have?"

I asked them if they had ever heard of that famous body-builder from ancient times known as Hercules. Every hand went into the air. They had all heard about Hercules and the amazing feats of physical strength for which he was famous.

"Well," I said. "You can call me SHERKULES (pronounced *SHERK-yoo-leez*)." Then they wanted to know if I was Mister Sherkules. And I said, "No, that's not necessary. Just plain old Sherkules would be fine."

Part of the fun of doing this took place in the hallways when I passed my students going to various classes. I would shout out, "Hello, Constantine!" and the student would shout back, "Hello, Sherkules!" Some other students, and teachers, too, would do a double take, wondering if they had really heard what they heard.

And so, my students were addressed by these names in class and they could sign these names on tests and exams. The only complication arose one day when I was under the weather and had to call for a supply teacher, but forgot to tell him about the ancient names. When he got to my grade eleven class, he passed a sheet of paper around the room to take attendance, and it came back to him at the front with nothing but ancient and medieval names. He thought the class was pulling a prank on him and was ready to send the entire class to the office. A student in the front row then showed him the instructions I handed out for their notebooks, explaining the purpose of having these names.

"If you put this list of names in Mr. Sherk's mailbox at the end of the day," the student said, "he will know who was here."

The supply teacher then relaxed and proceeded with the lesson.

Now fast forward to 2011, when I received an email from Alan Stewart, now living in Mississauga. He sent me the story of his 1961-or-thereabouts Austin Westminster he drove to high school, and I published the story in my weekly syndicated "Old Car Detective" column.

He mentioned that he had been a student of mine at Northern Secondary in 1972 ("You were the best history teacher I ever had") and reminded me that his name for that school year was Moses. He still remembered his ancient name thirty-nine years later. By this time, I had retired and had moved back to my hometown of Leamington, Ontario (the Tomato Capital of Canada). In November of '11, he was down this way on business and we got together for lunch. He not only remembered his ancient name, he also remembered that Spartacus sat in front of him, and to his right was Julius Caesar.

Alan Stewart also remembers their modern names. Henry Jahn was Spartacus and Mark Liddel was Julius Caesar.

18

Pronouncing Ancient Greek Names

When we reached the section on Ancient Greece in the grade eleven Ancient and Medieval History course, I spent a few minutes teaching the students how to pronounce the names of ancient Greeks we would be studying. Starting with a famous ancient Greek philosopher, I wrote the following name on the blackboard: SOCRATES.

At first I told them how NOT to pronounce it. It is not "*SAWK-ratz.*" It is "*SAWK-ra-teez.*"

I followed that name with a famous politician in ancient Athens, and I wrote his name on the board: PERICLES. It is not pronounced "*pair-IK-elz.*" The proper way is "*PAIR-i-kleez.*"

I then gave them the name of a Greek playwright: EURIPIDES. The wrong way is "*YUR-i-piedz.*" The correct way is "*yu-RIP-i-deez.*"

Then I told them that if they follow the pattern shown in the first three examples in which any names ending in *es* have to be pronounced as a separate syllable, they will probably be able to figure out how to pronounce any ancient Greek names as soon as they see them.

Then I said, "Let us imagine that we are going to study an ancient Greek who might have invented the jock strap. Here is how he spelled his name:

TESTICLES

"I will now count to three, and just after I get to three, I want all of you to shout his name out loud. Here we go now ... ONE ... TWO ... THREE!"

And they all shouted, "*TES-ti-kleez!*"

19

Where Has Ancient History Gone?

In one of my first years of teaching, a couple of my students rewrote the lyrics of the Peter, Paul, and Mary song: *"Where Have All the Flowers Gone?"* as a review for tests and exams. Re-written, it went something like this:

Where has ancient history gone, long time passing,
Where has ancient history gone, long time ago.
Where has ancient history gone, gone but not forgotten,
But never to return, but never to return.
Where has Hammurabi gone, with his famous law codes,
Where has Hammurabi gone, from Nineveh and Tyre.
Where has Hammurabi gone, in the Fertile Crescent.
North of the Persian Gulf, north of the Persian Gulf . . .
Where have all Phoenicians gone, with their cedars of Lebanon,
Where have all Phoenicians gone, as they sailed away.
Where have all Phoenicians gone, maybe circled Africa.
And reached Britannia's shore, and reached Britannia's shore . . .

These lyrics helped the students when studying for tests and exams. I know because I was supervising an exam one day and saw a student looking puzzled, as if trying to remember a correct answer. I tiptoed a little closer to his desk and heard him quietly humming one of the songs we sang in class. Then he smiled, stopped humming, and wrote something down. I surreptitiously peeked over his shoulder at his answer. It was correct!

20

The Story of Henry Heme

One of my favourite periods of history to teach was the span of 118 years when the Tudor family ruled England, from Henry VII in 1485 to the death of Queen Elizabeth I in 1603.

When Henry Tudor defeated King Richard III at the Battle of Bosworth Field in 1485, he became King Henry VII of England.

When he died in 1509, his son became the famous Henry VIII. When he died in 1547, his only son became Edward VI. He was nine years old at the time and died in 1553, when he was fifteen. His half-sister Mary then became Queen Mary I.

When she died five years later, her half-sister (all three children had the same father but different mothers) Elizabeth became queen and ruled for the next forty-five years, passing away in March 1603.

In all, there were five members of the Tudor family who ruled England from 1485 to 1603. To help my students remember the name and number of each ruler and in the proper sequence, I told them that I would give them six Tudor rulers for the price of five. And Tudor no. 6 was Henry Heme (pronounced *HEE-mee*). And he was the only member of the family with a telephone number: Tudor 7-8611.

I got the idea for Henry Heme's phone number from a hit song by the Marvelettes (the first Motown all-girl group) called "Beechwood 4-5789." It was released on September 1, 1962, stayed on the charts for seven weeks, and hit a high of no. 17. The song was so lively and catchy that I was still humming it four years later, even after I started teaching:

Henry Heme's first name stood for Henry VII (1485–1509). His second name ("HEME") stands for the first letters in the names of the other four Tudor rulers: Henry the Eighth, Edward VI, Mary I, and Elizabeth I. You can avoid getting the two *E*s mixed up by remembering that Edward and Elizabeth ruled England in alphabetical order.

The telephone number reminds us of the number that comes after each ruler: Henry the Seventh, Henry the Eighth, Edward the Sixth, Mary the First, and Elizabeth the First, hence Tudor 7-8611.

After ten years of adding "Henry Heme" to the grade nine British History course in my class, a student walked in one day and said, "Hi, Mr. Sherk. Hey, about that phone number you gave us in class yesterday. I called that number when I got home."

Horrified, I said, "You weren't supposed to call that number. It's just to help you remember the names and numbers of the Tudor rulers. So what happened?"

"Well," he said, "that number belongs to a farmer north of the city."

"And what did he say?" I wanted to know.

"Oh, he was pretty mad. He said he's been getting phone calls for some guy named Henry Heemee around this time of year for the last ten years."

"Well, don't call him again," I said.

Then I wondered if I should call the farmer and tell him I'm Henry Heme and ask if there had been any calls for me in the past ten years. But I didn't.

21

Master of Originality

By the end of my fourth year of teaching at Northern Secondary School, I had come up with several unusual and creative teaching techniques. For the two geography classes I taught in my first two years in addition to history, I created a character named Steve McKing (with apologies to the then-very-much-alive Steve McQueen of Hollywood fame) who rode a Phonda motorcycle (with additional apologies to Honda). Steve McKing rode his motorcycle all over the land masses we covered in the grade nine geography course, which at that time included Australia, New Zealand, Africa, and the British Isles. My students pointed out to me that he could ride his motor-cycle right across the Tropic of Capricorn without falling off because it was only an imaginary line on a map.

By my second or third year, I was handing out multi-coloured maps because I had discovered that "ditto masters" for our Gestetner copying machines came in red and green, as well as the standard bluish-purple. I traced an outline map of Hudson Bay and James Bay in red and then superimposed on it in green an outline map of the British Isles at the same latitude. My students were amazed to discover that the British Isles are that far north, warmed by the Gulf Stream, and that Hudson Bay is so big, it could swallow up England, Wales, Scotland, and Ireland.

I started every grade ten Canadian history class by passing a five-dollar bill around the room and I usually got it back. The course started in 1896 with the election of Canada's first French-Canadian prime minster, Sir Wilfrid Laurier. It's his picture on the five-dollar bill. Then I pulled out a ten to show them Macdonald and a twenty to show them the Queen. I suggested that the next time someone asks you if you can give them two fives for a ten, you should reply by saying, "Oh, you want two Lauriers for a Macdonald."

In an attempt to take an interdisciplinary approach to the teaching of history, I tried to make use of other subjects, such as mathematics. Two of my students in my grade ten history class that year actually designed an algebraic formula, which, they claimed, proved that the First World War had to break out in 1914.

Music was another subject lending itself to the teaching of history. We celebrated Sir John A. Macdonald's birthday every year on January 11 (he was born on a Wednesday in 1815) with the whole grade ten class singing the Canadian version of an old American Civil War marching song:

> *John A. Macdonald lies amolderin' in the grave,*
> *John A. Macdonald lies amolderin' in the grave,*
> *John A. Macdonald lies amolderin' in the grave,*
> *But his Canada nation marches on!*

I received a very pleasant surprise at the end of my fourth year of teaching when my 5A10A class bestowed upon me the degree of Master of Originality. I took it home and framed it and still have it.

These are the names of the students in 5A10 who signed the Master of Originality degree listed in the order in which they signed it (with apologies for any spelling mistakes):

C.M. (Cathy) Wilkinson	Barry Godden
BOSS	Mona Oikawa
V.K.C. (Karen) Alison	Charles Montgomery
J.M.B. (Jane) Gillett	Jennifer Rowe
H.B. Panczakiewcz	Brian Finlayson
Susan Green	Phil Ainsley
Fiona Lamont	Peter Harrison
Anne Kalin	Stuart Davis
Larissa Tachenko	Bill St. Germaine
Robert Correll	Heather Ritchie
Brian Mitchell	Margot Ritchie
Andy Kenins	John Ferguson
Pam Ingram	Steffi Balles
Jane Slaght	

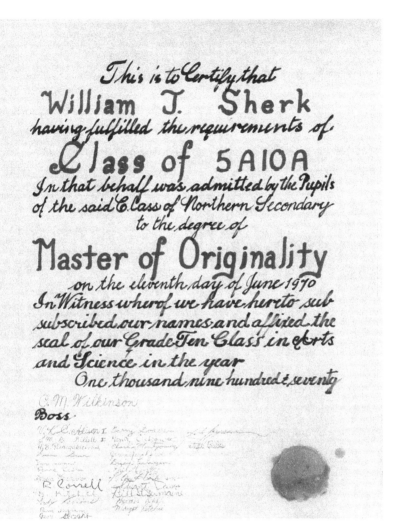

All the students in my 5A10A class of '69–'70 signed their names on my Master of Originality degree organized by Cathy Wilkinson (BOSS).

22

Marking ... Marking ... Marking ...

It was Monday and I was enjoying a corned beef sandwich in the teachers' lunch room with several of my colleagues when one of them (an English teacher) announced that he had spent the entire previous weekend marking papers. I don't know whether he was bragging or complaining, but that recollection got me thinking about my own experiences with marking.

I taught history and that subject lends itself to two basic types of tests: essay-style (one or more paragraphs in good sentence form), and objective (fill in the blanks, multiple choice, pin the name on the map, etc.). I was fond of giving quick little tests at frequent intervals, ideally every Friday based on the work of the week. These would consist of ten sentences with a blank in each. This way, I was testing their recall and also their ability to spell. And some of the ancient names, like Vercingetorix, were not as easy to spell as Tom, Dick, or Harry.

My classes had five rows of desks facing the front with about six students in each row. When I handed out test papers in my first year of teaching, I walked quickly down each row, handing out the papers facedown. But no matter how fast I did it, I could not see all my students at the same time, and I could not be sure if some of them succeeded in sneaking a peek at the paper before the test began.

Then I came up with the perfect solution. I walked over to the student sitting at the first desk in the first row and placed on his or her desk enough test papers upside down for that row. I instructed that student to place both hands on top of the test papers and press down hard to make sure they stayed upside down until the test started.

Walking backwards, I then gave the appropriate number of test papers to the students sitting at the front of the other four rows, along with the same instructions, all the while fixing all five of them firmly within my sight. There were now a total of ten hands pressing down hard on all the upside-down papers. Excitement was now building throughout the room!

Then I positioned myself alongside the first and second desk in row 5, which was closest to the window, and gave the following instruction to the students at the front: "Move one of the test papers to one side, while keeping it face-down. That will be your paper." I stood and watched them do this. "Now, on the count of three — WAIT FOR IT! — you will pass the other papers face-down to the person sitting behind you."

I paused, relishing the tension in the room. Some students actually leaned forward in anticipation. Then I said in a loud voice: "ONE … TWO … THREE!"

With a great flurry of paper, the tests began moving down each row face-down as I walked down the side of row 5 to follow their progress to the back of the room, all the while calling out those three magic words: "FACE-DOWN! FACE-DOWN! FACE-DOWN!" And as I was belting out these words, I had the entire class within my range of vision.

Next instruction: "PLACE BOTH HANDS ON TOP OF YOUR UPSIDE-DOWN TEST PAPER … and wait for the signal."

Now every student had a test paper face down on their desk. "Wait for it! Wait for it! … START!"

Another great flurry of paper, this time sounding like a flock of birds taking off or landing. "WRITE YOUR NAME AT THE TOP OF THE PAPER … YOUR NAME … AT THE TOP BEFORE YOU ANSWER ANY QUESTIONS!" I watched carefully to make sure all of them did this.

Silence now descended upon the room as the students proceeded to fill in the blanks. Two or three minutes were usually enough.

"TIME'S UP! Fold your paper over and write your name on the outside!"

Again, from my vantage point beside row 5, I could see the entire room and could see that every paper was being folded and a name written on the outside. For tests in my Ancient History classes, they were permitted to sign their ancient names, which they carried with them throughout the school year.

The test had now reached a critical stage. They were all written and folded over, but they were not yet in my hands. A dramatic delivery was required. I walked to the front of the room while instructing the student at the back of each row to stand up. I then instructed ALL the students to move their paper over to the edge of their desk, with a slight overhang over the aisle. I then told the students at the back of the room to crouch, as if ready to run the four-minute mile. They did as instructed.

I stared at them and the whole class from the front of the room ... paused ... then shouted while waving them in: "BRING THEM IN!" This is what happened next:

1. The five students at the back rushed up the aisles, scooping up the test papers one after the other and handing them to me at the front of the room: "Row 4 ... the winner! ... followed by row 1 ... now 3 ... now 5 ... and now 2" (or whatever the sequence happened to be).

2. Then I wrapped them with an elastic, tossed them into my gym bag, and introduced the next lesson.

Paragraph-style tests I usually gave on a Tuesday. That way, we could spend part of Monday's class reviewing the material. A typical paragraph-style test looked like this:

In good paragraph style, identify and explain the historical significance of any FOUR of the following (5 marks each) during the years that Sir Wilfrid Laurier was prime minister:

a) The Election of 1896
b) The Diamond Jubilee
c) Sir Clifford Sifton
d) The Boer War
e) The Alaska Boundary Dispute
f) The Election of 1911

I would give the class five minutes to look over their notes before the test. The test itself would occupy the next fifteen or twenty minutes. As soon as the test was finished, the papers were once again collected by the students at the back of each row and handed to me.

The next day was Wednesday, which brought the inevitable question: "Sir, do we get our test papers back today?"

"Not today," I would reply. "I assigned the test a week ago to give you a full week to prepare for it, and I'm giving myself the same length of time to mark them. I am planning to return them to you next Tuesday."

High school teachers know just how busy life can be while teaching six classes a day with as many as 195 students. Sometimes next Tuesday would arrive without all the test papers marked. I would tell the class on those occasions that I will not assign another test until all of the previous ones were marked and handed back. The inevitable reply was comforting to my ears: "Take your time, Sir! We can wait!"

For longer essays (five hundred words or more), the students wrote them at home and bought them to class by a deadline date (otherwise a late penalty was imposed). Some students padded their essays with vague and repetitious wording in order to meet the required number of words. Whenever I came across examples of this, I wrote the letters "B.S." in large red lettering across the page.

Some students complained about my use of those letters, claiming they were vulgar and had no place in a school essay. And I would reply, "I don't know why you are upset. The letters *B.S.* mean 'Be Specific.'"

23

The Great Bicycle Race

It was the early 1970s when Johnny Walker, principal of Northern Secondary School, asked me to be the staff adviser for the United Way campaign at our school. That is when I came up with the idea for The Great Bicycle Race.

Four teachers volunteered to form four teams to compete in a relay-style bicycle race around the track that circled the football field at the back of the school. A special assembly was called to give each team the opportunity to explain to the rest of the school why their team was the best and therefore why everyone should vote for them. Sponsor sheets were circulated through home form teachers and hundreds of dollars were pledged as students picked their favourite team.

That was in 1973. The race was still going strong three years later when the following report appeared in the 1976 Northern Yearbook:

"A stirring spectacle of speed and stamina transpired on Northern's new asphalt track on the sunny noon of October 22. Northern's third annual Great Bike Race was underway to raise hundreds of dollars for the United Way.

"The race was kicked off by the Wizard of Words, William Sherk. The running commentary was supplied by Jack de Bartok and Garth Mosbaugh from their lofty edifice high in the middle of centre field (compliments of N.S.S. Stage Crew and Julian Bowron Sound System Unlimited). The hard-fought race was ridden to the melodious strains of the Rubber Ducky Non-Marching Band which was snugly ensconced high in the stands.

"Ruth Crist and her balloon team sold helium-filled GBR balloons as other students sold steaming hot dogs and chocolate drinks to the avid spectators.

"Each team (led by a teacher with four students) was splendiferously bedecked in multi-coloured BIKE RACE T-shirts as they pedalled and ploughed around the track.

"The winner of the Silver Spoke Trophy was none other than 'Champagne' Charlie Chinchen and his team: Elizabeth Starr, Irene Dorosh, Kip Watson, Beyea and John Palmer, followed by Handlebar Harold Lass, Glenn Wayward Way, and Fearless Doug Fraser.

"Congratulations and thanks to all who rode and assisted."

W. T. Sherk

Following the second annual Great Bicycle Race in 1974, at a music concert put on by our school at Massey Hall, the Silver Spoke Trophy (designed and built by the students in the woodworking class at Northern) was brought out on stage on a purple cushion by Vice-Principal Stewart Scott, who presented it to the winning team while the school orchestra played a few bars of "Land of Hope and Glory."

Many years later, I visited Northern and saw the Silver Spoke Trophy on display in the front hall and was assured by one of the students that the Great Bicycle Race was still being held every year for the United Way.

The Great Bicycle Race of 1975 on the track behind Northern Secondary School attracted hordes of spectators eager to cheer on their favourite teams, ably assisted by several NSS cheerleaders. Mr. Chinchen of the History Department is mounting his multi-gear bike for another lap in this relay race to raise money for the United Way.

24

Robin Hood at Massey Hall

When I taught at Northern Secondary School, we had a dynamic head of the Music Department named Bill Toumon. During the 1974 Christmas season, he booked the school into Massey Hall in downtown Toronto for a special evening with the NSS band and orchestra. We sold lots of tickets and filled every seat in that two-thousand-plus grand old theatre, which was built around 1894.

Bill Toumon loved getting other staff members involved in his productions and when he approached you, it was very difficult to say no. He asked me to dress up as Robin Hood in green tights, a green tunic, and a quiver full of arrows over my shoulder. He wanted me to come out on stage at the start of the show, take an arrow from my quiver, and use it as a baton for leading the assembled crowd into a rousing rendition of "Jingle Bells."

The big night arrived and I was suitably attired for my part. I was even wearing a green felt hat of the style popular when Robin Hood and his merry men lived in Sherkwood (oops! That's Sherwood) Forest.

My big moment quickly arrived. Out on stage I strode to the microphone, welcomed everyone, and promised a magical night of wonderful music. "And now, let's all stand up and sing 'Jingle Bells!'"

The crowd rose to their feet and the orchestra swung into action as I pulled an arrow from my quiver and flourished it as a baton. I was conducting for the first time in my life! I felt a surge of power that quickly departed as I wondered why they seemed to be singing slightly faster than I was conducting. "I'd better move a little faster if I want to catch up to them," I thought to myself.

But that didn't help. The audience still sounded as though they were singing a little faster than I was conducting. Again, I increased my speed but to no avail. Now they were singing the song faster than I had ever heard it sung before!

I knew the song was going to end with "a one-horse open sleigh" but that sleigh must have been attached to a runaway horse. Almost before I knew it, the song was over. I bowed and stepped off the stage to make way for whatever was coming next.

I walked back into the wings and approached Bill Touman. He had a peculiar look on his face.

"What happened out there?" I asked.

And he set me straight. "Mr. Sherk, they were following you. All you had to do to get them to slow down was to slow yourself down."

No one has ever asked me to conduct again.

Here I am, dressed as Robin Hood at Massey Hall in the 1970s with an arrow I pulled from my quiver to lead two thousand people in a rousing rendition of "Jingle Bells" with disastrous results.

25

Reading the Dictionary One Page a Day

On Saturday, November 10, 1973, I was sitting at my desk at home and marking some essays on Ancient Egypt from my grade eleven students. One of those essays concentrated on the historical importance of the Nile Delta, that triangular part of the river near its mouth where it empties into the Mediterranean.

Suddenly, I became curious about the word "delta." I knew that the fourth letter of the Greek alphabet was also "delta" and wondered if there was a connection. I reached for my copy of *The Webster Universal Dictionary*, published in England in 1963. It was the dictionary my parents had given me when I was a student at university. I looked up "delta" and here is what I found:

> Delta: n. The fourth letter of the Greek alphabet, its form as a capital being a triangle. (Geog.) n. A triangular-shaped tract of alluvium at the mouth of a large river (e.g. Nile, Ganges) through which the distributaries of the river reach the sea.

I was fascinated to discover the connection between the Greek letter and a river delta. Then it occurred to me that a lot of other interesting information must be contained between the covers of this dictionary, if only I knew where to look. The only way to find all the other linguistic treasures would be to read the dictionary from cover to cover, one page every day!

I checked the number of pages (1205), grabbed a calendar, and quickly calculated that if I started right away, I could read the entire dictionary in three years, three months, and sixteen days. I would reach the last page on Saturday, February 26, 1977.

Starting with the *As*

I started right away, and even before I got to the bottom of the first page, I knew I would keep going to the very end. On page one, I found the word "abactor" (which I had never seen before). It means a cattle thief! But not just any cattle thief. An abactor is very serious about rustling. "Abaction" is "the stealing of a number of cattle at one time." It comes from Latin: *ab* (from) and *agere* (to drive). Imagine how helpful this word would be if you are doing some genealogical work on your family tree. You might find an abactor hanging from one of the branches.

On page two, which I read on Remembrance Day 1973, I found "abecedarian," one who teaches, or learns, the alphabet. That was another word I could not remember ever having seen before.

I returned to school on Monday and told my students about my latest project: reading a dictionary from *A* to *Z*. Almost every day, when I walked into the classroom from then on, at least one student would say, "So tell us, Mr. Sherk, what words did you come across last night? Find anything interesting?" My students were checking up on me to make sure I had been doing my homework!

I noticed on page six a word was missing. No mention of "a capella" (without instrumental accompaniment). I made a notation in the margin and checked a copy of the *Merriam-Webster Collegiate Dictionary*, where it was listed.

Three days before Christmas of 1973, I reached "antipodes" (*an-TIP-o-deez*), which sounds like the name of an ancient Greek. My copy of Webster's defines it as "regions directly opposite any given point on the globe." It's based on the Greek prefix *anti* (against) and *pous* (foot). It is often preceded by "the," and when we talk about the antipodes, we are referring to that part of the world inhabited by people whose feet are directly opposite ours. In other words, the bottom of our feet face the bottom of the feet of the people living at the antipodes. My students found this word fascinating.

It took until January 20, 1974, to get to the end of *A* and the start of *B*. I persevered, and learned a lot about our language as I went along. For example, under "awful" there are several meanings: "full of awe, filling with fear and admiration, impressive, venerable, majestic, solemn, dreadful, terrible, horrible, ugly, unsightly, extremely."

It was great fun teaching the building of St. Paul's Cathedral, designed by Sir Christopher Wren and constructed following the great fire of London in 1666. I told my students that it was built exactly the way he wanted it. And when it was finished, he stood back, looked at it, and said, "It's aweful!"

The students would look puzzled. "Why would he say it's awful if it was built the way he had designed it?" they wanted to know. I would keep repeating the word "awful" but now breaking it into its two syllables: "It's aw-ful. It's aw-ful."

Suddenly, a hand would go up. "I know, Sir! I know! He meant it filled him with awe! And today, we'd say it's awesome!"

Here come the *B*s!

On March 13, 1974, I encountered "boustrophedon," an adjective described as "writing alternately from left to right and from right to left, as with early Greek writing (from Greek: turning like an ox in ploughing). I gave my students the opportunity to write this way in class. They tried it and, like the ancient Greeks, abandoned it as too impractical. But it intrigued one of my fellow teachers, Bruno Scinto. Whenever we passed each other in the hall, he would say, "Mr. Sherk, how's your boustrophedon?"

My First New Word!

On December 1, 1975, I began chatting with a fellow teacher in fractured French after mentioning my journey through the dictionary. He was Bob Warren from the school's Guidance Department. Both of us had studied French in high school, but neither of us could claim to be bilingual. And yet we were not entirely unilingual, either. We had been exposed to a second language and still retained a smattering of it.

I was already familiar with the Latin prefix "sesqui" meaning one and a half, as in sesquicentennial (a celebration of 150 years, literally a century and a half). And so I turned to Mr. Warren and said, "Bob! Guess what! We're sesquilingual!"

Right away, I phoned a dictionary publisher and asked if they could put this very useful word into their next edition. That's when it was explained to me that dictionaries only included words already in use. If I want to see my new word join the English language, I would have to get it into circulation first.

Undaunted, I soldiered on with my dictionary reading and reached the last page right on schedule on Saturday, February 26, 1977. The last word in the dictionary was "zyxomma" (a dragonfly with large eyes and narrow head, found in India). It's a word very difficult to fit into everyday conversation in this part of the world.

Meanwhile, and because of the example of sesquilingual, some of my students took up the challenge to invent some new words of their own. Some fellow teachers on staff were also inspired to flights of neologistical fancy.

An Avalanche of New Words!

From my students:

Marilyn Finkler coined "baldephobia" (the fear of going bald).

Mike Bolitho coined "bubbliophile" (a lover of champagne, and similar in sound to "bibliophile," a lover of books).

Ray Nakamura coined "duodemilingual" (knowing two languages and part of a third).

Sam Rosenbaum coined "lectaquaphobia" (the fear of water beds).

Julian Bowron coined "Lexiconia" (an imaginary island in the middle of the North Atlantic where new words are manufactured).

John Cargill coined "outro" (the opposite of "intro" as in "We'll use this song for the intro and that song for the outro.")

SPECIAL NOTE: The British rock group Bonzo Dog Band recorded a song around 1971 entitled "Intro and Outro," showing they invented the word "outro" at least five years before John Cargill came up with it. However, as of 2003, the word "outro" was still not in the Merrriam-Webster Collegiate Dictionary. John Cargill could have coined the word independently of the Bonzo Dog Band (I had never heard of that group or that song until I started writing this book). Two people on opposite sides of the globe might each coin the same word because words are often coined to fill a need that is not yet covered in the English language. John Cargill, you still qualify as a budding neologist! Coined any other new words lately? Let me know.

More New Words ...

Dave and Garry Ballentine coined "quadocular" (wearing eyeglasses). They are both quadocular.

Roland Drake coined "quizbang" (a surprise test).

Glenn Wong coined "sesquigamist" (a person previously married and now engaged to be married again).

And Michael Granatstein coined "sesquisuit" (a suit with a reversible jacket).

And now some new words coined by my fellow teachers.

Bob Warren coined "cabloop" (to drive a cab by a roundabout route in order to raise the fare).

Gerry Dunlevie, vice-principal at North Toronto Collegiate, coined "omnibibulous" (fond of drinking all beverages). Mr. Dunlevie hastened to add that he is not omnibibulous.

And mathematics teacher Desmond Ottley coined "spork" (a spoon with fork prongs at the tip, often seen in plastic at fast food outlets). [Editor's note: this is a very common term/utensil now!]

All these words, and many more, appeared in my first two dictionaries, *Brave New Words* and *More Brave New Words*, both published by Doubleday Canada.

The first one went on sale in bookstores all across Canada on Friday, September 14, 1979, accompanied by a flurry of press releases, including this birth notice:

> SHERK — After spending the last 18 months in labour,
> Bill "Sesquilingual" Sherk is delighted to announce the

birth of his first book, BRAVE NEW WORDS, 'the newest, funniest and most original dictionary in the world' on Friday, September 14 at 12:01 a.m. This new arrival measures 5 1/2" by 8 1/4", contains 192 pages and weighs 9 1/2 ozs. It is already eating *blupper* (a single daily meal in place of breakfast, lunch and supper) with a *threek* (a fork with 3 prongs) and a *spork* (a plastic spoon with fork prongs at the tip, available at fast food outlets). Delivery performed by Doubleday Canada Ltd. and Alger Press. Book and author doing well.

That was thirty-three years ago. None have as yet caught on with the exception of "spork." All have yet to appear in a regular dictionary. And it often takes time for a new word to catch on. The world's first motel (the Motel Inn) opened on December 12, 1925, in San Luis Obispo, California, but the actual word "motel" (a contraction of "motor hotel" because you can drive your car right up to your door) did not appear in a regular English-language dictionary until 1950. People kept staying in tourist homes or tourist cabins all through the 1930s and 1940s because they were cheaper. And so it took the word "motel" twenty-five years to make the grade.

"Sputnik" got in much faster. The Russians launched the world's first artificial satellite on Friday, October 4, 1957. The word "sputnik" (Russian for "fellow traveller") hit newspapers all over the world. A dictionary publisher in New York saw the word, realized its importance, and called long distance to the company's printing plant in the American Midwest and dictated a definition of "sputnik" over the phone. The very next day, that dictionary was printed, permitting us to say that "sputnik" landed in an English language dictionary in less than twenty-four hours.

Nine years later, I started teaching. When I asked my class one day if they knew what the word "sputnik" meant, most of them opted for a Russian potato.

Now a final word about my journey through the dictionary from *A* to *Z*, a journey that spanned nearly three of the final years I taught at Northern Secondary and the first several months of my time at North Toronto Collegiate. On November 18, 1998 (a year after I retired), I received an email via North Toronto Collegiate from a former student from the 1970s who was now living out west:

> Dear Mr. Sherk: I've forgotten most of the history but I'll never forget some of the words you taught me in class. You must have been in the 'C' section of the dictionary in those days because I remember seeing the words CAPRICIOUS and CAPACIOUS scrawled on the board in huge letters.
>
> Today I am the mother of a nine-year-old daughter with dyslexia who is a writing fiend and storyteller. She can't spell, but she writes up a storm for an eager audience. My eight-year-old son is a history buff who fancies himself a rap singer. All I can say is, I wish you could teach my children too! Thanks for everything.
>
> Helene Meurer, Salt Spring Island, B.C.

26
Catching a Streaker...

Remember streaking? You ran naked through a public place with a bag over your head. It was a surefire way to get attention, and it became a popular fad during the early 1970s. It even inspired a hit song, "The Streak," by Ray Stevens, climbing to no. 1 on the charts for three weeks (May18–June 7, 1974).

Several streakers chose Northern Secondary School as the place to streak. And some, maybe all of them, were believed to be students at the school. It was difficult to identify them from the neck down, but we were certain that all the streakers were boys.

Members of the staff at Northern were asked to keep their eyes and ears open (especially their eyes) for any news of an impending streak. Another teacher and I were stationed one day behind a stack of old desks in a hallway in the basement leading off from the cafeteria. According to one of our vice-principals, the word on the street was that a streaker was planning to run naked through the cafeteria at lunch hour. The other teacher and I were supposed to grab him (grab him where?) as he hoped to escape by running into the hallway where we were hiding.

We crouched behind the desks and commiserated with each other on what we were doing. "We spent four years at university and end up doing this?" or words to that effect. We waited and waited and waited …

Finally, the lunch period ended and students headed off to their afternoon classes with no sign of the streaker. The vice-principal came around and relieved us of our duty. But he urged us to be constantly vigilant and to report any suspicious movements immediately to him.

We never heard anything more about it. And, like any other fad, streaking ran its course and was replaced by mooning (pulling your pants down in public and showing everyone your bare behind while wearing a bag over your head, then pulling your pants up and running away).

I was teaching at North Toronto Collegiate in the 1980s when three students mooned an entire assembly, then ran out the back door. See page 151 for the full story.

27

See This Piece of Chalk?

My history teacher for Ancient and Medieval History when I was a student in grade eleven at UTS was Andy Lockhart, a great teacher full of enthusiasm and with a gift for conveying his love of history to his students. I was fortunate in having Mr. Lockhart as my teacher again several years later, when I attended the Ontario College of Education after graduating with an honours degree in history from York University (with a University of Toronto degree). He was my history professor at OCE, and he was now teaching us how to be good teachers! What a wonderful luck to have had him as a teacher and later as an instructor on the techniques of good teaching. He was a natural at it.

Among the things he taught us was this: start each class by deliberately saying or doing something to grab their attention. This was excellent advice, and also a great challenge if you tried something different every day for the 198 days of the school year. I remember applying his advice in many different ways. Using a piece of chalk, for example.

I would get the students seated and make sure their notebooks were open to copy that day's date off the blackboard. Then I would hold up a fresh piece of chalk and tell them to look closely at the tip. They would stare at it, wondering what I was up to. I would move it around and watch their eyes follow it. I would tell them that today's lesson has been compressed onto the tip of the chalk by a revolutionary new teaching technique. Whenever the tip of the chalk comes in contact with the blackboard, it would automatically start to write today's lesson on the board. I would then demonstrate by bringing the chalk into contact with the blackboard, and I would write the title of the lesson on the board with my hand apparently doing nothing more than holding it in place while it did its work. Some students looked skeptical, but I ignored that.

Then we would launch into the lesson itself and I would say no more about the chalk. It had served its purpose. It grabbed their attention.

28
Spelling Mistakes

It all began one day when I was handing back essay assignments to my students. I circled every spelling mistake with a red pen and deducted half a mark from the total for every mistake. Naturally, of course, they complained about this and thought it qualified as "cruel and unusual punishment." Always eager to listen to what they had to say, I compromised by saying I would only deduct a maximum of three marks (equivalent to six spelling mistakes) from their essay in order to reduce the penalty.

The mention of spelling mistakes often triggered off one of my favourite lessons. I always took great delight in discussing with my students the fact that the English language is very un-phonetic when it comes to the way we spell our words. Consider knee, sword, and pneumonia, all of which have silent letters. There is even a silent p in swimming, but that's a different matter altogether.

My students who had difficulty with spelling often expressed a wish that our language should change its spelling so that the spelling matches the pronunciation. That way, mistakes in spelling would be a thing of the past because, if you knew how to pronounce a word, you would automatically know how to spell it. For example, the word "beautiful" could be changed to "beeyootiful" and I as their teacher would not have to use so much red ink because their spelling would be perfect.

At this point in the lesson, I would mention the famous British philosopher and writer George Bernard Shaw, who passionately believed that our entire language needed an overhaul so that spelling matched pronunciation. If that happy day should arrive, students would not have to memorize the proper spelling of words and could concentrate more on learning whatever it is they want to learn.

To dramatize the wild and crazy spelling patterns in our language, Shaw deliberately misspelled an ordinary, everyday word to draw attention to the need for reform. I would write on the blackboard the word he deliberately misspelled: GHOTI.

I would then ask my students how they think it should be pronounced. No one came even close in figuring out the ordinary, everyday word that can be spelled as "ghoti." Finally I put them out of their misery and gave them the answer: FISH.

Now for the next question to my students: How can the letters GHOTI possibly be used to pronounce the word FISH?

It wasn't long before the students figured it out. Someone would point out that the GH in GHOTI produces the "F" sound as in rough, tough, and cough. Someone else would point out that TI in GHOTI comes from the SH sound in ration, nation, and sanitation.

Explaining the O pronounced as an *I* usually took a little longer — until a student would excitedly say, "Sir! I've got it! I've got it! The *O* comes from the sound of the short *I*, like in WOMEN!"

"Correct!"

I was raised on *Archie* comic books back in the 1950s (*Archie* was first published in February 1942, just three months before I was born!), and today I see Archie Andrews is still very much alive and on sale at check-out counters in supermarkets. I'll never forget the story of Moose (one of Archie's pals), who had trouble with spelling but was the star of the football team at Riverdale High. Anxious to help him keep up his marks in order to stay on the team, the principal, Mr. Weatherbee, administered a spelling test to Moose. He would be given a word, and if he got even ONE LETTER correct, he would pass.

"Moose," said Mr. Weatherbee, "spell coffee."

Moose scratched his head, furrowed his brow, and slowly but surely spelled the one word that, hopefully, would keep him on the team: "K-A-W-P-H-Y." I think the team lost their next game.

Around 1450, Johann Gutenberg began using moveable type for the printing of books, and the world since then has never been quite the same. The arrival of the printing press did away with handwritten Bibles (which took months or even years to copy by hand) and all other handwritten works. Suddenly the world of the Middle Ages was turned upside down with this new outpouring of knowledge.

But even with the arrival of the printing press, spelling was still not standardized. In Shakespeare's day (1564–1616), you could spell a word any way you wanted to, and Shakespeare himself reportedly had thirteen different ways of spelling his own name. Back in those days, if you knew only one way to spell a word, you were considered not very well-educated.

Many of the early printers in England had come over from Holland, and Dutch spellings inevitably crept into the books they were printing in English. The "u" in guest and the "h" in ghost are two examples of this.

Those early printers liked to have what printers call "right justification," that is, the margin on the right side of the page should be as straight as the margin on the left. It looked better, most people would agree, and I drew my students' attention to this in their textbook.

"And how did the publisher of our textbook line up every line on the right perfectly straight?" I would ask. I could usually count on a correct reply: "Sir, the printers probably have a machine that does that for them automatically."

"Yes," was my reply, "but back in the old days, when no one had a machine like that, was there still a quick way to do it, without altering the spacing of every single letter and word?"

A short silence usually followed this question as they pondered possible answers.

Sometimes they needed a clue to help them along. "Remember, way back in bygone centuries, there was no such thing as standardized spelling. You could really spell any word any way you wanted …"

A hand shot into the air. "Sir, if you alter the spelling of words on a page to fit the length of the line, that would do it!"

"Correct! Early printers simply altered the spelling of words to make each line longer or shorter as required. As a result, in some old books, you can find the same word spelled several different ways on the same page!"

In 1755, Dr. Samuel Johnson of London, England, published his famous *Dictionary of the English Language* after seven years of labour. It was an immediate bestseller, and not just because people were curious about the proper spelling of words. England was growing rapidly in wealth by the mid-1700s, thanks to overseas explorations, and many English people eagerly embraced the opportunity to rise to a higher social, educational, and economic standing. Helping them do this was the good doctor's new dictionary. By reading it carefully, you could cultivate the proper use of the language, and this could ease your entry into the higher classes.

"Now copy down the definition of the word 'window' in the new dictionary," I would say to my students as I wrote it on the board: *An orifice in an edifice*, suggesting that Dr. Johnson was not without a sense of humour.

At a very proper literary tea just after the dictionary was published, some very proper English ladies came up to the now famous lexicographer and said, "Oh, Dr. Johnson, we are so glad that you saw fit not to include any vulgar words in your dictionary." To which he wittily replied, "And I see, dear ladies, that you have been looking for them."

But even with the publication of Johnson's impressive dictionary, people still mispronounced words, and this continues today. My first dictionary was published in 1979, making me a lexicographer just like Dr. Johnson, and it was titled *Brave New Words*. It contained one hundred main entries of new words that were not yet part of the English language (see Chapter 25 for a detailed account of its contents, much of which was supplied by my students).

The entry relating to our discussion of spelling mistakes was "pekilar," defined as any mispronounced word. "He'll never get voted into office. Every speech he gives is full of pekilars."

On the next line, which indicates etymology (the source of the word), we read: "Coined by accident in 1849 in the Red River Colony on the site of present-day Winnipeg, Manitoba."

The commentary I wrote on "pekilar" is worth repeating here:

"If you're looking for a Greek or Latin root for 'pekilar,' you're wasting your time. This word was born in a little schoolhouse in the Canadian West over a hundred and fifty years ago. In his book, *The Selkirk Settlers in Real Life*, R.G. MacBeth tells us how it happened:"

> ... the success or failure of a teacher (in the Red River Colony) was decided by the inspection and report of the trustees aforesaid. As these trustees were for the most part "plain, blunt men" whose ... dialect was more or less affected by Gaelic, Salteaux, Cree, and French influences,

the lot of the teacher was not always a happy one. When Inkster was teaching in '49, the trustees came to inspect, and one of them gave to the leading class in the school the word "pekilar" to spell. It had never been heard of up to that time, and so proved a "poser" for the whole class from head to foot, whereupon the trustees grew somewhat indignant and threatened to dismiss the teacher whose leading class could not spell "pekilar." The teacher, however, asked to see the word, and saved his official head by pointing out that it was pronounced "peculiar," which latter word was triumphantly spelled by the class, who thus vindicated the scholarly attainments of their teacher.

When time permitted, I would ask my students if any of their family names had changed in spelling over the years. I gave my own family name as an example, which began in Switzerland and gradually changed over here:

Schoerg became Scherck, which later became Sherk, often because my ancestors did not know how to spell their own name and immigration officials often took a guess as to the correct spelling. Some students gave similar examples.

A final word or two on spelling mistakes. Every once in a while I would come across one or two that made me laugh. Here are a couple: the Romans wore scandals on their feet; the Pheasants Revolt broke out in England in 1381.

29

September a Special Month

September is an exciting month for students and teachers. There is the excitement of seeing so many people after being away for two months. The weather is still nice and the courses are fresh and new.

I always wrote the day's date at the top of the blackboard so the students would have a good reason for opening their notebooks right at the start of class. I was glad that September was the first month of the new school year because it gave me an opportunity to teach something in the first minute of the first day.

While they were copying down September 7, 1994, for example, I would underline the first four letters of September. Then I would ask the class what *sept* means in French. Many students had already studied French before they came to me, and the question was easily answered. *Sept* in French means "seven."

Then I would ask, "Do you see anything unusual in the number seven being part of the month of September?"

Then a hand would go up. "Sir, September is the ninth month in our calendar, so why is the number seven in there?"

"Good question," I would reply. "Can anyone suggest an answer? And while you're thinking about it, consider the month of October. An octopus has eight legs because *octo* means 'eight' but October is our tenth month. And November is based on nine and December is based on ten, giving us the decimal system, even though they are the eleventh and twelfth months."

A student would soon hit upon the answer. "Maybe our calendar at one time had only ten months and January and February were added later on."

That is exactly what happened. The old Roman calendar, from which ours is heavily derived, had only ten months until two extra months were added at the beginning. All the other months were shoved ahead two places but the names remained the same.

Until the Emperor Augustus (31 B.C.–14 A.D.) renamed the month of his birth in his name (hence August), that month was *sextilis* (the sixth month in the old calendar). And Julius Caesar, not short on conceit, but very short on modesty, had already named July in his honour, thus displacing the former *quintilus* (meaning fifth month).

You can be sure that around everyone's dinner table at home at the start of a new school year, the parents will ask, "Well, what new and exciting things did you learn in school today?"

And I can hear the reply: "We learned something really cool about the month of September …"

30

Memory Power

In October 1976, I rented a large meeting room on the second floor of Northern District Library, just down the street from North Toronto Collegiate. I created a course called MEMORY POWER to help people improve their memory, and I designed a yellow flyer with black printing, which I circulated all through the North Toronto area.

Forty-two people signed up for the course, which ran for two hours every Wednesday evening for five weeks. The fee was $20 and the course totalled ten hours. The people who signed up were adults from all walks of life, as well as some high school and university students.

When I called the roll on opening night, only forty-one people were there. I jokingly suggested that the one person who had pre-registered and had not shown up had perhaps forgotten that this was the opening night of the course designed to assist people in remembering things.

At the start of the second week's class, a woman showed up who had not attended the opening session. She gave me her name — she was the one who was missing the week before! She was very embarrassed and said she forgot all about it last week.

I said, "This is the perfect course for you!"

I based the course on three principles I obtained from one of Dale Carnegie's excellent books. He said there are just three ways we remember things:

IMPRESSION
REPETITION
ASSOCIATION

I told my class about one of my fellow students who attended the Glendon Campus of York University when I was an undergraduate there in the early 1960s. He was rushing to the Leslie Frost Library on campus to return an overdue book when he ran right into one of the glass doors and ended up in the hospital for a couple of days. That glass door obviously made a strong IMPRESSION on him because he never ran into it again.

When we were very young, we learned our ABCs by reciting the letters of the alphabet over and over and over again until we knew them all in alphabetical order. This constant REPETITION made it possible for us to learn all our ABCs all the way from *A* to *Z*.

Then I pointed out that if you take the first letter of the three magic words (IMPRESSION, REPETITION, and ASSOCIATION), those letters spell IRA, which could remind you of the Irish Republican Army. Just remember IRA and you will remember the three magic words.

Many of the students were eager to improve their ability to remember names. With forty-two people in the class all interested in doing this, I started by asking them to introduce themselves to four people sitting near them, and to ask those people for their names.

Then I asked them to ask again, and be sure to say their names out loud as soon as they give it to you.

Meanwhile, while they were talking to one another, I circulated around the room because I wanted to learn ALL their names as quickly as possible, and by using the three methods described by Dale Carnegie:

IMPRESSION

REPETITION

ASSOCIATION

In class, we just concentrated on first names. If a man's first name was Don, I would ask him if he lived anywhere near the Don River in Toronto. Simply by discussing that question with him, it brought his name to my attention and helped me to remember it.

If a woman's first name was Dorothy, I would ask if she had seen the 1939 film classic, "The Wizard of Oz," in which Judy Garland played the role of Dorothy Gale. Again, more conversation based on the person's name.

Some students already had a way of helping others remember them. A lady named Erica said, "Bill, you will always remember my name by thinking of Miss America."

I replied, "Yes, Erica, and you can remember my name by thinking of the end of the month, when all the bills come in."

These techniques (IRA) were of enormous help to me when meeting six new classes of teenagers every September. First, I would pick up the alphabetical list of students from the school office and look it over before meeting the class. That way, I could spot any names that might be difficult to pronounce, and also see if any names popped up twice or more.

Then it came time to meet each class. I had the room arranged so that the students would sit in five rows of desks facing the front. When they first came in, they would sometimes gravitate toward the back of the room. I would then stand at the first desk at the front of each row and inform the students in that row to fill up all the empty desks between them and the front of the room.

Next I would start to take attendance by calling out each name on the class list. I would stand at a podium at the front of the room while doing this so that I could fill out a seating plan while taking attendance. As soon as each student indicated they were there, I would mark their name in the appropriate square on the seating plan, with their first name larger than their last name.

I would make a point of repeating their name and also asking them if they preferred a shortened version of their first name (e.g. did Michael prefer Mike or his full name when being addressed in class?).

I did not rush through the taking of attendance. This was a very important step in learning their names.

When that was finished, it came time to issue their textbooks. I would call them up to the front, about three at a time, to pick up their textbook and sign for it. While they were doing that, I would walk back and forth at the front of the room, glancing at the seating plan, then at the class, then at the seating plan, then at the class … memorizing where each one was sitting.

When everyone had their textbook, I would tell them to mark their name in it at the front and then take a couple of minutes to browse through it, thereby giving me more time to study the seating plan and walk around the room while memorizing their names.

Two minutes before the end of the period, I would direct their attention to the board at the front of the room, where I had written my name.

I would say, "All of you know my name, and now I want to make sure I know all YOUR names. I will go down each row and call out your first name, and if I make a mistake, please correct me because I want to learn all your names as quickly as possible."

At this point, I had their total and undivided attention because they had never before encountered a teacher claiming to be able to learn all their names on the first day of school. And I deliberately made a production out of it. I started by calling out: "ROW ONE," then went down that row and pointed to each student while calling out their name.

Hastening back to the front of the room, I said, "Next I will do ROW TWO."

And I did.

"Now for ROW THREE ..."

"Now for ROW FOUR ..."

"And now for ROW FIVE!" When I got to the end of that row, with all names correctly called out, I said, "Now we know each other!"

Almost always, the class burst into a spontaneous round of applause. Then the bell would ring and off they would go to their next class. It was a nice way to start the new school year.

My Twenty-One Years at North Toronto Collegiate Institute

31

Arriving at North Toronto

Leaving Northern Secondary to go to another school in October 1976 was difficult for me because, after ten years there, the school had become like a second home and the teachers were like a second family. But the prospect of higher pay (as assistant head of history at North Toronto Collegiate) and being two blocks closer to home proved irresistible.

On my first day at North Toronto Collegiate, I knew by the end of my first-period class that I was going to enjoy this new school. The day's announcements came over the PA system into each classroom and they were read aloud by students taking their turns in front of a microphone in the school office on the first floor (I was on the third). The announcements began this way:

"Tuesday, October 12, 1976, and welcome to the Hot Air show!"

I had started teaching my Memory Power course (see page 99) the previous Wednesday evening at Northern District Library, and now had to adjust to a new school during the day while teaching a new course at night. My Memory Power course included techniques for helping people remember other people's names, and I applied those techniques in getting acquainted with my sixty-five fellow teachers at North Toronto Collegiate.

I visited the staff room on my two spare periods and at lunch every day and introduced myself to any teachers sitting nearby. I also asked them for their names and wrote them down in my log book. I learned the names of about five or six teachers a day. By the end of October, I knew them all and they knew me.

32

Are You "Sesquilingual"?

I coined my first new word ("sesquilingual" — knowing one language and part of another and based on the Latin prefix *sesqui* — one and a half) while I was still teaching at Northern Secondary School. That word inspired my students to coin other new words. Less than a year later, I was teaching at North Toronto Collegiate, where the word-coining frenzy continued.

So many new words came my way that I wrote three dictionaries of new words, all published by Doubleday Canada. And it all began with "sesquilingual," a very impressive-sounding word. Nine times out of ten, if you tell people you're sesquilingual, they'll say, "My gosh! You mean you can speak six languages?" But it was one-and-a-half languages that John Fraser of the Toronto *Globe and Mail* had in mind when he reviewed the French play, *The Trojan War Will Not Take Place*, on May 6, 1977:

> It is done in French, although the company provides a free earphone set that gives a fairly tortured running translation. If you're a "sesquilingual" dummy like me, you'll find yourself leaving the set on only for the difficult longer speeches and gratefully turning it off when you can make your own language connections — or, more to the point, acting connections.

Fraser put quotation marks around *sesquilingual* because he first saw the word a few days earlier in a letter I had written to the editor of the *Globe and Mail*. Fraser (who later became the *Globe*'s Peking, now Beijing, correspondent) assured me that when he uses the word again, he will omit the quotation marks.

The two other daily papers in Toronto also took note of the word-coining fever. Elaine Carey, *Toronto Star* staff writer, penned "Are You a

Sesquilinguist?" on December 29, 1976, earning for that paper the first recorded use of the word in print. Connie Woodcock of the *Toronto Sun* wrote: "What's the Good Word" for April 3, 1977, highlighting the new words popping up from local neologists.

Meanwhile, several of my students jumped aboard the word-coining bandwagon and came up with several spin-off words from sesquilingual:

Bill Weir coined "sesquiguous" for something which is only slightly ambiguous. For example, "We're having a turkey for dinner tonight" (which could mean a turkey is one of the dinner guests or, more likely, a turkey is on the menu).

John Calvin concocted "sesquiphonic" for a sound followed by an echo (disc jockey in echo chamber: "Folks, this program is coming to you in sesquiphonic sound!").

Other students wondered if they would lose marks by using any of these new words in, for example, an English essay. I told them that if they put any of these words in quotation marks, as John Fraser did, that tells the teacher that you know the word is not an official word.

See also "Reading the Dictionary One Page a Day" page 82.

33

Letter from Pierre Berton

In the 1970s, Pierre Berton and Charles Templeton could be heard daily on Toronto radio station CKEY (580 AM) for a five-minute dialogue. I encouraged my students to listen to them discuss and argue a wide range of current topics, and it amazed me that Pierre Berton seemed to have an opinion on everything!

Apparently, this exasperated Charles Templeton one day because he accused Berton of having too many opinions. Berton shot back, "I have opinions because I'm paid to have opinions!"

The late Pierre Berton, author, journalist, raconteur, and radio and TV personality (1920–2004) took the time to write (or rather type) a letter to me postmarked July 14, 1977, in response to a letter I had written to him the previous January. The letter itself disappeared years ago. I showed it to everyone I knew and someone must have made off with it as a souvenir. But I still have the envelope and I still remember what the letter said:

> Dear Mr. Sherk: Thank you for your letter re *sesquilingual*. I am happy to find out what I am. I apologize for the delay in answering your letter of several months ago. I have been busy writing my latest book and everything else has to wait.
>
> Yours truly,
> *Pierre Berton* (his actual signature).

My letter to Berton was prompted by one of the daily dialogues on CKEY, in which he admitted that he was not bilingual, but did know a few words in French. Aha! That would mean he was sesquilingual. Off went my letter around January 1977 and I received his reply nearly six months later (the postmark is July 14, 1977).

A few years later, I had the pleasure of meeting Pierre Berton, who was the guest speaker at a conference of history teachers at a hotel near the Toronto airport. We briefly discussed my new word and once again, he said he was happy to find out what he was.

PIERRE BERTON

21 Sackville Street
Toronto, Ontario M5A 3E1

Mr, Bill Sherk

Word Power Instructor *89 Castleknock Rd.*

York University

4700 Keele Street *Toronto*

DOWNSVIEW Ontario M3J 2R6

Continuing Education

34

Two Visits to Stonehenge in One Day

In the first unit of the grade nine British History course, we studied the daily life of the ancient Britons, and of course the megalithic masterpiece known as Stonehenge, constructed on the Salisbury Plain in southern England some 4,000 years ago, and still partially standing today.

A film arrived one day in the North Toronto Collegiate history office entitled *Stonehenge*. It was a sixteen-minute, sixteen-mm movie in black and white. I had a seventy-minute class coming up in a few minutes, and decided to show the movie twice. At the start of the class, I announced, "There will be a test tomorrow on a topic we haven't covered yet."

The inevitable response: "Sir, how can we be tested on something we haven't covered?"

"We'll cover it now," I replied. "Now close your textbook and notebook and face the front of the room. I will now show you a short movie. Do not take any notes during the movie. As soon as the movie ends, you will open your notebook and write down everything you can remember from the movie."

Then I turned on the projector and turned off the lights. It was a charming little movie with diagrams. When it was over, I said, "Now you have ten minutes to write down everything you can remember from the movie, and your notes should include some diagrams."

I gave them between ten and fifteen minutes to do this. Next I told them, "Double up with a partner and check each other's notes to see if you can find something extra to add to your own notes."

This took another few minutes. After that, I announced, "Like the seventh inning stretch at a ball game, stand up and walk around the room for the next two minutes."

When I got them seated again, I said, "Now I will show you the movie again, and this time you can have your notes open to add any details you think are still missing."

The second viewing of Stonehenge took us to within two minutes of the bell. I then said, "When is our next test?"

"Tomorrow," they replied.

"Didn't hear you. What did you say?"

"Tomorrow!" they shouted.

"And what will it cover?"

"Stonehenge."

"Louder, please."

"Stonehenge!"

"Louder!"

"STONEHENGE!"

Then the bell rang and the class was over.

I am happy to report that on the test the next day, their marks ranged from eighteen to twenty out of twenty.

35

"Stayin' Alive" in the Stone Age!

In the late 1970s, disco dancing became a widespread craze all over North America, thanks in large part to the release of the motion picture *Saturday Night Fever* starring John Travolta.

The Bee Gees composed and sang many of the songs on the soundtrack, including the opening number *Stayin' Alive*. The title of that song inspired me to create a new assignment for my grade eleven Ancient and Medieval History students.

I wrote the instructions on the blackboard before the class arrived and covered them up with a pull-down map. After I took the attendance, I announced that we would be going on a field trip (cheers and clapping!) … but without leaving the room (boos and groans!).

"I will start playing a song," I said, "and at the same time I will show you your instructions on the blackboard. You have till the end of the song to copy them down. Here we go!"

The tape recorder was cued right up to the first note. I pressed the button and yanked on the map at the same time to roll it up out of the way. Here is what they saw and copied down off the blackboard:

> You and everyone in your row will be sent back in time to the Stone Age for 30 days. You will meet in a corner of this room to prepare yourself for this adventure. You will discuss with your fellow time travellers what you will have to do to stay alive here in the Toronto area 10,000 years ago. One of you will record the comments and suggestions from the group, and the group will then select someone to be the spokesperson to report to the rest of the class.

While they copied this down, the Bee Gees were blasting away with their hit song.

When the song ended, everyone had the instructions copied down. Then each row of students went to a corner of the room to put together how they would stay alive in the Stone Age for the next thirty days.

Their reports to the rest of the class revealed a time in prehistory no one wanted to live in! The search for food might take all day. And where would they sleep at night? In a cave? Lucky if you can find one that isn't already occupied by other humans or by wild animals. And if it starts to rain?

The bell rang at the end of the class, bringing us happily back to the present. *Patterns in Time* was an alternate textbook we had for the Ancient and Medieval course. I always enjoyed bringing the introduction of that book to the attention of my students. It said:

> If the age of the Earth (around four-and-a-half billion years) were compressed into a single calendar year, the first eight months would be devoid of any life and the next two months would have only very primitive animal forms. Human beings would not appear until sometime between 10:00 and 11:00 p.m. on New Year's Eve, and only in the final minute before midnight would they learn how to grow grain. The momentous developments of the last one hundred years would all occur during the last second.

36

Hi-Jinx 1979

During the years I taught at North Toronto Collegiate, the school hosted a spectacular Open House every two years. It had been decided before I came there that every other year was better than every year because a lot of work was entailed in putting it on, and everyone would make a greater effort if it was held every other year.

The name of the Open House was "Hi-Jinx," a name that went back to the days of the students' parents. The evening featured a fashion show, puppet show, environmental display, art show and sale, photography exhibition, bake sale, various sports events, and a chemistry magic show.

A highlight of the evening that got everyone revved up was the big variety show in the auditorium. Here is the report I wrote for the yearbook:

> Lights! Curtains! Action! At precisely 7:15 p.m. on Friday, January 26, the 1979 edition of Collegiantics burst into action with an unparalleled display of talent and entertainment never before seen anywhere! From the foot-tapping "Seaside Rendezvous" and "Roller Skate Rag" to the hand-clapping "Hi-Jinx Hoedown," the audience revelled in the richness of costume, song, dance, skit, and drama. "The Charleston" and "Boogie Woogie Bugle Boy" took us back to a bygone era.
>
> Sweeping us into the current entertainment scene was "Last Dance" and the fourteen-member "Summer Nights." Mr. Krueger's Klodhoppers supplied the OOM-PAH-PAH while the Six Pistols supplied the punk rock. "Romeo and Juliet" served up a slice of Shakespeare hot on the heels of Steve Lewarne giving us a slice of "American Pie." And who could forget John Egan's Magic

Show or John Burry's impression of Mr. Rogers? The NTCI Stage Band hit a home run with "Take Me Out to the Ball Game" and Kelli Hurst revived those thrilling days of yesteryear when, dressed as the Lone Ranger, she played the William Tell Overture on her teeth!

To the MCs (Christine Dixon, John Burry, and John Egan), the Stage Crew, the performers, staff advisors Mr. McCarron, Mrs. Love, and all the others who helped make the show possible, many thanks! We played to a combined audience of nearly two thousand people and we helped the school raise over four thousand dollars. Don't miss our next Collegiantics Show. Curtain time is the end of January 1981.

John Egan's magic show was unforgettable. Even today, over thirty years after seeing it on stage, I can still remember how he wowed the crowd. For his first stunt, he made a glass of water disappear. He filled the glass with water from a pitcher and held it high in the air for all to see. Then an assistant placed a large towel over his head and upper body. The towel lifting up slightly on one side could mean only one thing. He was drinking the water! With a drum roll, the towel was quickly removed. He held the glass upside-down to show the water had disappeared, and took a bow to a thunderous round of applause.

His next trick was even more demanding. He held a towel in front of himself, which concealed his body from his waist to his feet. He then lifted the towel up just enough to show he still had two legs. "I will now make one leg disappear!" he claimed with suitable bravado. Down went the towel and both legs were covered up. Then he lifted the towel up to his knees and he was standing on only one leg. Where did the other leg go?

Where indeed! He had to bring it back before making the other leg disappear, which he did, just like the first. Then he brought both legs back again to an even louder round of applause!

For his finale, he held up a yardstick, the kind that teachers have in their classrooms to point to details on a pull-down map. He made a bold claim: "I will turn this single piece of wood into two separate pieces!"

Everyone held their breath, wondering how — or even *if*— he could do it. Holding the yardstick with a hand at each end, he turned his back to the crowd, raised one knee, pulled up on his hands to the sound of splintering wood, and turned again to face the crowd. He proudly held aloft not one, but TWO pieces of wood. If memory serves me correctly, that trick won him a standing ovation!

HI-JINKS!

Lights! Curtains! Action! At precisely 7:15 pm on Friday, January 26, the 1979 edition of Collegiantics burst into action with an unparalleled display of talent and entertainment never before seen anywhere! From the foot-tapping "Seaside Rendezvous" and "Roller Skate Rag" to the hand-clapping "Hi-Jinx Hoedown", the audience revelled in the richness of costume, song, dance, skit, and drama. "The Charleston" and "Boogie Woogie Bugle Boy" took us back to a bygone era. Sweeping us into the current entertainment scene was "Last Dance" and the fourteen member "Summer Nights". Krueger's Klodhoppers supplied the OOM-PAH-PAH while the Six Pistols supplied the punk rock. "Romeo and Juliet" served up a slice of Shakespeare hot on the heels of Steve Lewarne giving us a slice of "American Pie". And who could forget John Egan's Magic Show or John Burry's impression of Mr. Roger? The NTCI Stage Band hit a home run with "Take Me Out To The Ball Game". And Kelli Hurst revived those thrilling days of yesteryear when, dressed as the Lone Ranger she played the William Tell Overture on her teeth!.

To the MC's (Christine Dixon, John Burry, and John Egan), the Stage Crew, the performers, Mr. McCarron, Mrs. Love, and all the others who helped make the show possible, many thanks! We played to a combined audience of nearly two thousand people and we helped the school to raise over four thousand dollars. Don't miss our next Collegiantics Show. Curtain time is the end of January, 1981.

Bill "Sesquilingual" Sherk

As well as the Collegiantics Show, Hi Jinks consisted of a fashion show, puppet show, environmental display, art show and sale, photography exhibition, bake sale, various sports events, and a chemistry magic show.

Article as it originally appeared in the 1979 NTCI yearbook, with pictures from the show.

37

"See You Later, Exfiltrator!"

In 1981, Doubleday Canada published my second dictionary: *More Brave New Words: The Latest, Newest, Funniest, and Most Original Dictionary in the World*.

The main entry on page sixty-six is *exfiltrate*: "To escape in small numbers from enemy territory without being detected. (Latin: *ex* — out of; Old French: *filter* — a strainer or filter). The opposite of *infiltrate*." It was coined by Canadian ambassador Kenneth Taylor after engineering the escape of six American diplomats from Tehran in January 1980. This dramatic event led to a lively discussion in my history classes, where we always kept a close eye on the daily newspapers to witness history in the making.

While these diplomats were escaping from Iran, I was working on the manuscript for *More Brave New Words*. As soon as I saw Ken Taylor's new word in the daily newspaper, I added *exfiltrate* as a main entry in my new book.

After it was published, I attended a conference of history teachers at a hotel near the Pearson Airport in Toronto. The guest speaker was Kenneth Taylor!

He held us spellbound while relating the details of exfiltrating the six Americans from Iran by way of the Canadian Embassy. When he finished speaking, I was invited to come up on stage and join him at the podium, where I presented to him an autographed copy of my new book, *More Brave New Words*. I also brought along my own personal copy of the book and asked him to autograph the page where his new word appeared. He wrote:

"Bill: See you later, Exfiltrator! Ken Taylor."

38

Five Hundred Years of New Words

Following the publication of my second dictionary, *More Brave New Words*, in the fall of 1981, I decided to tackle new words from another angle. My friend Ron Hill (also a teacher for the Toronto Board) showed me his copy of a condensed version of the *Oxford English Dictionary*, which he and his wife had purchased from their local Loblaws supermarket in Mimico (now part of Toronto).

"You bought this in a supermarket?" I asked. "That seems like a strange place to buy a dictionary."

Ron explained that it was a special promotion to encourage you to buy all your groceries at that location. Whenever you bought a certain dollar value of groceries, the store gave you the first installment of your dictionary — letter by letter. And so Ron and Jane headed home with all the *A*s, then all the *B*s, then all the *C*s, and so on. They literally ate their way through the alphabet. And when they reached *Z*, the store gave them a special binder to hold all the pages.

I began flipping through this dictionary and noticed that beside each word, and in bold type, was the earliest known year that each word had appeared in print. Suddenly it struck me, after having written two dictionaries of brand new words, that every word in the English language was at one time brand new!

When I discovered that the word "America" was coined in 1507, I decided to write a dictionary unlike any other in the world. All the main entries in my dictionary would be arranged not in alphabetical order, but in chronological order! But could I find a new word for every year from 1507 up to the present?

Ron Hill's dictionary filled the bill until I reached the years close to the present, which his did not cover. I checked the *Barnhart Dictionary of New English*, which brought me much closer to the present. Doubleday planned to publish *500 Years of New Words* in the spring of 1983, and I wanted to include a new word for 1983. I got it off the radio in January of that year: "dermizip" (a surgical zipper that takes the place of stitches after an operation).

With the book coming out in the spring of 1983, it would not cover five hundred years, but only 476. To make the contents match the title, I added a special section at the end entitled "The Shape of Words to Come," containing twenty-five new words that I was convinced would join the English language sometime in the future.

Reprinted now for the first time in twenty-nine years are twenty-five words that are still waiting for official status in the English language. Many of these were coined by my students and fellow teachers:

Après-puck: a social gathering after a hockey game (compare après-ski).

Bladderclock: The use of the urinary bladder as an alarm clock. Drink lots of water before going to bed and you'll never be late for school.

Cybrow: A person whose eyebrows are joined together (from the Cyclops: one-eyed giants in Greek mythology). Coined by Matt Trowel, Toronto.

Deplasticate: to rob someone of all their credit cards. Richard Johnston, Islington, Ontario.

Examnesia: loss of memory while writing an exam. Lois Grant, Calgary, Alberta.

Friend-in-law: a friend you met through your in-laws. Jonathan Lovat Dickson, Toronto.

Fuzztache: A "peach fuzz" moustache on a teenager before starting to shave. Mario Bartoletti, Toronto.

Klickage: a new metric replacement for mileage. Earnest McCallum, Sawyerville, Quebec.

Leapian: A person born on February 29.

Meanderthal: A wandering cave man or woman. William French, *Globe and Mail.*

Noctrinesia: The inability in the morning to remember the brilliant idea you had in the middle of the night. Harold Lass, Toronto.

Pump-a-lunch: A combination gas station and restaurant. "Eat here and get gas!" Vera Mooney, Victoria, British Columbia.

Smatterlingual: Knowing one language and a smattering of others. Tom Fulton, Toronto.

How many of these words will catch on to become a permanent part of our language? Only time will tell.

39

Get Ready for a "Sherkout"!

In August 1984, I was driving in Toronto by myself, going I can't remember where, when a song I had never heard before came on the car radio. It was so lively and upbeat, I pulled over to the side of the road, climbed out, and danced all around the car with the radio blaring at full volume. It was the new big hit by Wham! called "Wake Me Up Before You Go-Go."

School would be starting in another couple of weeks and I decided then and there at the side of the road that I would add an aerobic exercise to all my history classes.

We would work out to the beat of fast music, starting with the song by Wham! I would tell all my students that their marks would improve by doing this because the extra oxygen going to their brain would make them more alert and better able to absorb all the material in the course.

The first week of school in September is pretty hectic, so I waited until halfway through the second week to spring it on them. I brought a boombox into the room, then climbed up on my desk at the front of the room, and told them all to stand up.

I told them what we were going to do, and I took them through a couple of manoeuvres before we started the music. I said that once we get into the song, we will point our forefingers toward the window and move our hands for four beats, then swing toward the door and do the same, then point toward the ceiling and do the same, then point toward the floor and do the same, all the while chanting at the top of our lungs the four magic words: "WINDOW! DOOR! CEILING! FLOOR!"

The poetic qualities of the chant were obvious: "window" and "ceiling" each have two syllables and "door" rhymes with "floor."

I then instructed a student to press the button on the boom box while everyone in the class struck a John Travolta-style *Saturday Night Fever* starting pose. I told everyone to follow what I'm doing (that's why I was standing up on the desk) and issued a challenge: "Keep up if you can!"

The music began and it was loud! We did the chant several times, then I added a few more moves that we later called the "windshield wiper," the "bow and arrow," the "chicken," and the "semi-circle." We also stretched toward the ceiling to the beat of the music as I shouted "Stretch! Stretch! Stretch! Stretch!"

Every student in the class was doing it with unbridled enthusiasm! And we were all in sync. If someone had walked in just then and saw the whole class doing it, they wouldn't believe that we had never done it before. It was incredible!

The students were soon referring to these aerobic workouts as "SHERKOUTS" and the news of what we were doing spread like wild-fire throughout the school. I realized this very quickly from the curious comments I got from other teachers in the staff room and because of what happened the following month when the school launched its annual fundraising for the United Way.

Each home form had to come up with a fundraising project. My home form printed flyers and distributed them to all the other home forms announcing that they were "renting" me out to perform Sherkouts for other classes in the school. Every class that booked a Sherkout then had to take up a collection after the performance and donate that money to the United Way.

By now, we were working out to a vast array of upbeat songs, including: "Honky Tonk Man" by Dwight Yoakam, "Heaven in My Hands" by Level 42, "Living in a Box" by a group of the same name, "When Smokey Sings" by ABC, "I Fought the Law (and the Law Won)" by the Bobby Fuller Four, "Never Gonna Give You Up" by Rick Astley, "School Days" by Chuck Berry, "I Don't Like Mondays" by the Boomtown Rats, "Freedom" by Wham!, "Always on My Mind" (the dance version by the Pet Shop Boys), "Lucille" by Little Richard, "Whole Lotta Shakin' Goin On" by Jerry Lee Lewis, "Hound Dog" by Elvis, "Walkin' On Sunshine" by Katrina and the Waves, "Long White Cadillac" by Dwight Yoakam, "Help Me Rhonda" by the Beach Boys, "All My Loving" by the Beatles, and many more!

I kept the windows open, except in the dead of winter, whenever we did a Sherkout so the students would have the benefit of fresh air while going through the manoeuvres. This meant, of course, that the music could sometimes be heard in other classrooms. That was usually never a problem, but the phone in my room rang one day during a Sherkout. I jumped off the desk and answered it while still leading the class in the moves. It was Dave Wallace calling from the room below to say, "Hey, Elvis, can you tone it down a little? Your students are shaking the ceiling in my room and my students are trying to write a test and dust is falling off the ceiling and onto their test papers."

I told him I would take care of it right away. I climbed back up on the desk and assumed a frozen position. The whole class froze. Then we continued the Sherkout just by moving our fingers and nothing else, not even our hands. It was the most amazing Sherkout I think we had ever done (even Michael Jackson would have been envious) and it kept the dust off the test papers in the room below.

Most of my classes were on the third floor, but I met my American History students in a seminar room in the basement. We were nicely into an extra loud Sherkout when I heard a pounding on my classroom door. Through the small window, I could see the face of Dr. Surender Kumra, who taught science in the next room. "Be with you in a minute!" I yelled, not wanting to stop the Sherkout until the song ended.

Student-drawn cartoon of me leading a Sherkout in the 1995 North Toronto Collegiate Institute yearbook.

When the music stopped, I climbed down off my desk and stepped outside into the hall, bracing myself for an angry blast. Instead, he said, "Ah, Mr. Sherk, I could hear the music all the way down to my room and so I came to investigate. After seeing what you were doing, I want you to come down to my Science class and do for them what you just did here, and I will stay with your class until you get back."

How could I say no? I carried the boom-box down the hall and into the Science lab. Instead of a desk at the front, there was a big, long counter with sinks and Bunsen burners and other scientific paraphernalia. I straddled two burners to get into a starting position, then away we went to the beat of the music. They all took part and the only problem I had was with the manoeuvres that took our hands high up over our heads. My hands kept hitting the panels in the ceiling and bouncing them up and down to the beat of the music. Then I returned to my class.

One day, three girls in my grade ten Canadian history class came into the room all excited. They had choreographed a Sherkout at home over the weekend to a lively, upbeat song and wondered if they could lead the next Sherkout.

"A great idea!" I said. "How about right now?"

They had brought a boom-box with them and I stepped aside so they could get into position at the front of the room. Then, with a signal from me to turn on their music, they stood on my desk and launched into their Sherkout.

After about fifteen seconds (and maybe because they were nervous doing it in front of the whole class), they got completely confused and out of sync. They motioned for me to turn off the music, which I did. From the look on their faces, I could see how disappointed they were and I could think of only one way to save the day. I called them over into a corner where we could talk quietly without the other students hearing us.

I said, "Here's what we'll do. You get back into position and I'll go to the back of the room. When the music starts, I'll lead the Sherkout from the back of the room and you three will be the only ones who see me. You do exactly as I do and the rest of the class will follow you."

And that's what we did. I'm sure the rest of the class thought the Sherkout was originating with the three girls, and everyone followed them in perfect sync to the end of the song.

I was chatting with Ken Olsen one day in the staff room. He taught English on the third floor right next to my room. He told me he had given his class some work to do at their desks and noticed that one of his students seemed a little sleepy and tired. Mr. Olsen slowly approached the student's desk to see if he was all right and heard him mutter to himself, "I sure could use a Sherkout right about now."

Sometimes, when time allowed, we did two Sherkouts, one right after the other. I wouldn't tell the class we were doing two. I'd jump off the desk at the end of the first song, then jump up just before my feet reached the floor so I would land noiselessly out of respect for the class in the room below, then walk toward the OFF button on the boom box. I knew another great song would start in another two seconds, and away we'd go again!

News of my Sherkouts eventually reached the ears of the principal, Jim Hogarth. He came to my classroom one day, wanting to know what these Sherkouts were all about. My students and I gave him a demonstration, and he, being a former physical education teacher, happily joined in. He was so impressed that he gave me a half-day off school later that week to drive out to Scarborough and perform a Sherkout for his wife's students at the school where she taught. The photo on the next page of me in action was taken in Pauline Hogarth's classroom.

As I got older (I was forty-two when I did the first Sherkout), I found I couldn't keep up the frantic pace for two songs and so from then on did only one. On those days when I was really feeling my age (early fifties), I'd start the Sherkout two minutes before the end of the period. The bell would ring in the middle of the song and the class would leave while dancing their way out into the hall. Eventually it was something I saved for Friday's class as a way to celebrate the arrival of the weekend.

When I retired in June 1997, several students asked me to do one final Sherkout at the farewell assembly with the entire student body there. How could I say no? I led the biggest Sherkout of my career with some eight hundred students following all the moves from where I was standing up on stage. The song I ended with was the same song I started with thirteen years earlier: Wham!'s big hit, "Wake Me Up Before You Go-Go."

About a year after I retired, I received a letter in the mail that had been sent to the school, and the school forwarded it to me. It was from the only student I had who was not able to participate in the Sherkouts because he had a heart condition (I wish I could remember his name and where I put his letter). His health problems apparently continued after he completed school. Here is what I remember reading in his letter:

> Dear Mr. Sherk: I was a student in one of your history classes at North Toronto Collegiate a few years ago and I remember how you used to lead the class in your famous Sherkouts. Earlier today, I heard a song on the radio that reminded me of you and those days. It was "Wake Me Up Before You Go-Go" by Wham! When I heard it, I did something I haven't done in a long time. I smiled.

40

Elvis: Live from the Grave!

In January 1985, I was persuaded (or maybe I persuaded myself) to volunteer for a staff part in the upcoming variety show called Collegiantics at North Toronto Collegiate. This show was held every other year and was a means of showcasing the variety of talent in the school. We had a student who played the harmonica with his nose (and heaven help him if he caught a cold just before his big night) and a girl who could play "Popcorn" on her front teeth.

I decided to give it a shot so that at least one member of the staff was in the show. Elvis had been dead for eight years, contrary to frequent sightings of the King at fast food outlets, and so Ian Waldron, head of the English Department and director of the show, put me on the program as "Live from the Grave!"

I had to wear an Elvis wig and fit myself into a white Las Vegas jump suit with a belt adorned with a giant buckle featuring an American eagle. I was glad the Americans chose the eagle as their national bird instead of the turkey, as Ben Franklin wanted them to. A belt adorned with a turkey would kill my act before the first note of the first song.

A student asked me why I thought I could pull it off — impersonating the King of rock 'n' roll. I told her I had seen Elvis LIVE at Maple Leaf Gardens on April 2, 1957, when I was in high school. It was his only visit to our city. She seemed impressed, but maybe she was just being charitable.

The big talent night arrived and the auditorium was packed with students, parents, grandparents, neighbours, and other teachers eager to see a history teacher make a fool of himself.

In preparation for my performance, I did something that the King of rock 'n' roll never had to do. I packed the front row with girls from my grade ten history class. They were there as "screamers" in case everyone else sat in total silence.

I paced back and forth behind the curtains as other acts preceded me. Some were good and some bombed. *Oh well*, I thought. *I won't be alone if I flop.*

Finally, my big moment arrived. I could hear Ian Waldron warming up the crowd at the mike, "And now, ladies and gentlemen, as you know, a baby boy was born in Tupelo, Mississippi, in 1935. The family moved to Memphis, where he recorded a song for Sun records and went on to become the most famous entertainer since the dawn of time!"

The crowd was going wild! How could I possibly live up to their expectations? The members of the stage crew rushed me into position just behind the curtains as Waldron cranked things up to a fever pitch: "And now … LIVE FROM THE GRAVE … (he had to shout at this point to make himself heard) … the KING of ROCK 'N' ROLL!!!"

With "Hound Dog" blasting from the loud speakers, I gyrated back and forth along the runway that jutted out from the stage and halted mere inches before the end while lip syncing the lyrics. My screamers did not let me down. They shrieked so loud, they almost completely drowned out the members of the audience who were laughing hysterically. Next song was "Don't Be Cruel." More gyrations, for which I paid dearly the next day. I knelt down and reached out to some of the screamers, almost, but not quite touching their outstretched fingers.

When the song ended, more screams. I finished with "Can't Help Falling in Love With You" while tossing brightly coloured kerchiefs into the crowd. When the last note ended, I was plunged into darkness as pre-arranged by Mr. Waldron. That was my cue to run behind the curtains to clear the stage for the next act. I disappeared with screams and applause ringing in my ears.

And then … a surprise ending!

I watched the rest of the show from behind the curtains, then got back into my street clothes, and made a hasty departure out the back door. I walked out to Yonge Street and into the McDonald's close to the school for a cold drink while wondering if Elvis ever got thirsty after a performance. As soon as I entered, I saw dozens of students in there who began screaming "ELVIS! ELVIS! ELVIS!" I pretended not to know them as I worked my way through the crowd and up to the counter, where I quietly ordered a 7-Up. When I turned around, they were all gone.

I carried my 7-Up outside and saw all of them standing on the sidewalk. "Hey," I said, "how come all you people left in such a hurry?"

One of my students stepped forward and said, "Sir, while you were ordering your drink, the manager came running out of his office and motioned for all of us to get out! Apparently, when we started yelling 'ELVIS,' he thought we might wreck the place."

And so the evening came to an end on a somewhat unexpected note (no pun intended). I looked up at the sky and didn't see Elvis, but thought he would be pleased, knowing that a high school history teacher imitating him could come close to causing a riot.

Incidentally, after Elvis left Toronto in 1957, he headed for Ottawa and wanted to stay at the Chateau Laurier. He was refused accommodation because the hotel manager thought his fans would wreck the place.

Dr. Surender Kumra (NTCI Science Department) invited me to join with him in performing like a pair of rock stars at a school dance in the 1980s. We rocked the house to the beat of "Wake Me Up Before You Go-Go" by Wham!

North Toronto Collegiate Institute Archives via Nancy Baines.

41

Were You Born in Farch?

My Effective Writing class at the Glendon Campus of York University in the fall of 1985 consisted of an especially enthusiastic bunch of students from all walks of life and all age groups. When the course ended, the students wanted it to continue!

Not able to arrange that, I suggested we get together somewhere early in the new year to celebrate. One of the students, Irene Tysall, offered her house where we gathered on a Saturday evening in early February, and several students brought their spouses or "significant others." At some point in the evening, the talk turned to new words, and someone said to me, "Bill, what do you think about *Farch* to replace February and March? If we had only one month between January and April, the winter might go faster!"

I can't remember who concocted this new month, but we were already into the first couple of weeks of Farch. I wrote this new word on the blackboard and told my students it was made up of two other words. Could they guess what those two other words might be?

In no time at all, they figured it out. "Mr. Sherk, Farch is a contraction of February and March!"

Then I asked for a show of hands. "How many of you were born in Farch?"

Half a dozen hands went up. Some students thought the new month was a great way to speed up the passage of winter, but others didn't like it because they enjoyed skiing and wanted the winter to last longer.

We then returned to our course of study for the rest of the period. Farch was quickly forgotten. Or was it? When the bell rang and the students were heading out of the room, I heard one of them say to another, "I can't wait to get home and tell my parents I was a Farch baby!"

[Editor's note: My friends throw a Farch party every year …]

42

Memorizing "High Flight" and Other Poems

I had the good fortune to have Ronald Ripley as my grade eight teacher at UTS. He believed in the importance of memorizing poetry, and I'm glad he did because I still remember some of the poems we memorized in his class.

Here's an example of a poem by the Canadian poet G.K. Chesterton. It was a very unusual poem because it talked about Jesus riding into Jerusalem on Palm Sunday from the viewpoint of the animal he was riding on. Here is how it went, as I remember it:

The Donkey

When fishes flew and forests walked,
And figs grew upon thorns.
Some moment when the moon was blood,
Then surely I was born.
With monstrous head and sickening cry,
And ears like errant wings,
The devil's walking parody
Of all four-footed things.
The tattered outlaw of the earth
Of ancient, crooked will
Starve, scourge, deride me — I am dumb,
I keep my secret still.
Fools! For I also had my hour,
One far, fierce hour and sweet.
There was a shout about my ears,
And palms before my feet.

Some churches recite this poem on the Sunday before Easter.

When I taught grade eleven Ancient and Medieval History, I required my students to memorize "Ozymandias," a sonnet written by Percy Byssche Shelley in 1818 (whose wife, Mary Shelley, wrote *Frankenstein*):

Ozymandias

I met a traveller from an antique land who said:
Two vast and trunkless legs of stone
Stand in the desert. Near them on the sand
Half sunk a shattered visage lies
Whose frown and wrinkled lip and sneer of cold command
Tell that its sculptor well those passions read
Which yet survive, stamped on these lifeless things,
The hand that mocked them and the heart that fed.

And on the pedestal these words appear:
"My name is Ozymandias, king of kings.
Look on my works, ye mighty, and depair."
Nothing beside remains. Round the decay
Of that colossal wreck, boundless and bare
The lone and level sands stretch far away.

We studied the building of the great pyramids along the west bank of the Nile. They are all on the west bank to symbolize the afterlife. By memorizing "Ozymandias," the students not only learned an important piece of poetic history; they were also reminded that the passage of time can turn powerful empires and mighty rulers into dust and decay.

I required all my grade ten Canadian history students to memorize "High Flight" by John Gillespie Magee. He was a pilot in the Second World War who was shot down and killed in 1941. When his belongings back at the base were gathered up, someone found a poem he had written on the back of an envelope containing a letter he had received from his mother. He never lived to see his poem become one of the best-loved poems in the English-speaking world. President Reagan recited it as his tribute to the seven astronauts who died in the *Challenger* explosion of 1986.

It's remarkable that the poem makes no mention of war, even though he must have written it when the war was raging. The poem simply describes the exhilarating feeling of freedom experienced by a pilot:

High Flight

Oh! I have slipped the surly bonds of earth
And danced the skies on laughter-silvered wings;
Sunward I've climbed and joined the tumbling mirth
Of sun-split clouds and done a hundred things
You have not dreamed of. Wheeled and soared and swung
High in the sunlit silence, hovering there,
I've chased the shouting wind along
And flung my eager craft through footless halls of air.

Up, up, the long delirious burning blue
I've topped the windswept heights with easy grace
Where never lark or even eagle flew,
And while with silent lifting mind I've trod
The high untrespassed sanctity of space,
Put out my hand and touched the face of God.

We talked about the poem in class, then I told my students to take it home and memorize it. When they came to class the next day, they wrote it out from memory and I collected it and marked it.

I remember one particular year when the next day rolled around and a student, Judy Barbeau, came into the room and said, "Oh, Mr. Sherk. You have made my dad so happy."

"I have?" I said with some surprise. "I don't think I've ever met your dad. What have I done?"

"Well, I took the 'High Flight' poem home last night and worked on it after supper, and when I thought I had mastered it, I went downstairs and asked my dad to look at it while I recited it out loud. I did, and it was perfect. Then he said to me how happy he was that I have you for my teacher. You see, my father had a teacher when he was in high school who had him memorize that very same poem."

43

Where Do You Come From?

I occasionally employed the lecture method of teaching with my senior history classes, partly to cover a lot of information in a short span of time, and also to accustom them to the lectures they would encounter at college or university.

For grade twelve Modern European History, we brought three classes together, thanks to a folding partition that converted two small rooms into a large one. Here is where I delivered one of my favourite lectures each year: "The Copernican Revolution." This all began in the 1500s when the Roman Catholic Calendar then in use (named after Julius Caesar and in use since 46 B.C.) had by A.D. 1500 fallen several days behind.

Most people at that time believed the world to be flat and in the centre of the universe, with the sun, planets, and stars revolving around it. That concept was about to change.

In his search for a more accurate calendar, Polish astronomer Nicholaus Copernicus made very detailed observations of the planets and stars without the aid of a telescope (it had not yet been invented). He was troubled by the retrograde motion of the planets. At this point, I quickly sketched some diagrams on the board to illustrate this phenomenon because at certain times of the year, the planets appeared to move in one direction and in the opposite direction at other times.

Copernicus searched through some ancient Greek manuscripts to see if someone else had tackled this same puzzle. He discovered that an ancient Greek had made the astounding suggestion that maybe the Earth moves around the sun instead of the other way around.

Copernicus found this made more sense and his book was published on his deathbed in 1543. The accuracy of his observations permitted Pope Gregory XIII to introduce the Gregorian Calendar in 1582 (the one we follow today). Yet at the same time, the Roman Catholic Church still clung to the Earth-centred view of the universe until 1822.

Meanwhile, other astronomers built upon the work done by Copernicus. Galileo turned a telescope toward the heavens in 1609 and saw four moons circling the planet Jupiter — a solar system in miniature. Johannes Kepler proved that the orbits of the planets were elliptical and not circular. And Sir Isaac Newton formulated the laws of gravity, which kept everything in the heavens moving in their proper path.

Near the end of my lecture, I mentioned the space ships from Earth that have now landed on Venus and Mars, and what we have learned about our two closest planetary neighbours in recent years.

I concluded my lecture by going back to the beginning and telling my students that, in a very real sense, the planet Earth is still in the centre of the universe. But how can that be?

The Earth is not in the physical centre of the universe, but it is our home and we almost always measure planets and stars in terms of how far away they are from our own planet, especially now that we are sending space probes beyond the limits of our own solar system.

If we ever land on some far-off distant planet and find intelligent life and a means of communicating, the first question they will ask is: "Where do you come from? Where is the one place in this vast universe you call home?"

I finished by saying the planet Earth is the only home we have and we would be wise to take good care of it.

44

From Model T Ford to Mustang Convertible

The grade ten history course covered Canada in the twentieth century. One of my favourite units was the section devoted to the automobile and how it changed the way we live. The Ford Motor Company was incorporated on June 16, 1903, and Henry Ford began building cars in Detroit with engines supplied by the Dodge Brothers. These engines were delivered to the Ford factory on wagons hauled by teams of horses.

Just one year later, Ford of Canada was born when the Ford Motor Company took over a wagon factory in Windsor, Ontario, and began building cars not only for Canadians, but other motorists throughout the British Empire.

While other early manufacturers of automobiles were building expensive vehicles for the wealthy, Henry Ford kept working toward a car so simple and so cheap that almost everyone could afford to buy one. These efforts culminated in the introduction of his famous Model T (he had used up most of the alphabet with earlier models) in October 1908.

The last Model T was built in May 1927. During its nineteen years of production, over 15 million were built. I told my students that a number of years ago, a man named Les Henry was the curator of the Henry Ford Museum in Greenfield Village in Dearborn, where the world headquarters of Ford is still located. Mr. Henry estimated the survival rate of the Model T at 2 percent. In other words, 98 percent of all Model Ts built no longer existed. They were scrapped or simply rusted away in farmers' fields.

At this point, a student would usually remark, "Well, Mr. Sherk, with that many now gone, I guess there aren't very many left."

"Let's do the math," I said. I would write 15,000,000 on the blackboard, then multiply that by 2 percent, giving us the number of Model Ts still around at three hundred thousand.

I gave my class a slide show on antique cars, which included several pictures of Model T Fords. I would love to have brought a Model T Ford to school, but I could not find the owner of one willing to bring it to the school so the students could look at it up close.

So we did the next best thing. I took them out to the school parking lot to show them a car that was built by the same company that built the Model T. I took my class to have a look at the car I was currently driving — a 1989 Mustang convertible. The students stood in a large circle around the car along with their pens and paper. Then I asked them what this car had in common with Henry Ford's legendary Model T.

A hand would go up. "Mr. Sherk, your car is black, and Henry Ford said you could order a Model T in any colour you wanted as long as it was black."

"Yes," I would reply, "and why was Mr. Ford so fond of black?"

Another hand would go up. "Because of the assembly line that he introduced around 1914. He was building cars so fast, the only paint that would dry fast enough was a black Japanese enamel."

"Now, any other similarities between the Model T and this Mustang?"

"Yes," came a quick reply. "Both cars were built by the same company, the Ford Motor Company."

"Very good," I would reply. "Anything else?"

"A lot of Model Ts had a folding top, especially the early ones. And your car also has a folding top."

"That's right," I would reply. "Now let's measure the wheelbase." Out would come my retractable tape measure and we would measure the distance between the centre of a front wheel to the centre of a rear wheel. It was exactly one hundred inches. "And, as we discussed in class, what was the wheelbase of a Model T Ford? All in unison now …"

The entire class would shout: "One hundred inches!" Then we had someone with a pocket calculator convert that into metric.

At this point, I would walk around to the driver's side of the car and casually reach in and place my hand on the steering wheel. "What other similarities do you see between the Mustang and the Model T?"

"They both have the steering wheel on the left!" someone would shout.

"And why is that significant?" I would ask.

Someone else had the answer: "You told us that when Henry Ford started building the Model T, most cars back in 1908 had the steering wheel on the right so the driver could keep a close eye on the ditch. But with Henry Ford's dream of a universal car, he put the Model T's steering wheel on the left because he figured the day would come when it was more important to watch the oncoming traffic than it was to watch the ditch."

"Very good," I would say, while reaching further into the car and resting my hand on the instrument panel. "Any other similarities?"

A hand shot up. "I know! Both cars have dashboards!"

"That's right," I affirmed. "And do you remember where the word 'dashboard' comes from?"

"Yes! In the days of horses and buggies, a board stuck up at the front to protect the passengers from the mud thrown up by the hooves of the horse. The mud would be dashed against the board instead of against the passengers, so it was called a dashboard!"

"Correct! Now let's look at some differences." I would walk to the left rear fender of the car and point to the gas-filler door.

I took possession of my new black Mustang convertible in the spring of 1989. If this was a black Model T Ford, I would be photographed sitting on the running board. With no running board on the Mustang, I did the next best thing: I sat on top of the door.

"I know!" said a student. "Your gas tank is at the back, but the Model T gas tank was under the front seat. And your car needs a fuel pump to draw the gas from the back to the engine, but a Model T had no fuel pump at all because it had gravity feed."

"And what if you were driving a Model T up a hill?"

Another hand in the air. "You would have to drive up the hill in reverse because the gas will not flow uphill by itself. Also, your car has a water pump and oil pump. The Model T had neither one for many years."

And so it went. We spent about half an hour looking the Mustang over (and under the hood) and talking about how it differed from and how it was similar to the Model T. My Mustang was built sixty-two years after the last Model T Ford rolled off the assembly line, and by the same company.

45

The Grapes of Wrath

On May 5, 2011, Lady Catherine (to whom this book is dedicated) and I had the pleasure of visiting the Avon Theatre in Stratford, Ontario, to see the stage adaptation of John Steinbeck's classic novel, *The Grapes of Wrath*, published in 1939 and depicting the plight of migrant famers in the United States in the 1930s. She treated me to this as a birthday gift (I had turned sixty-nine the day before). I have read the book twice and have several times seen the 1940 screen version starring Henry Fonda. The book itself won Steinbeck the Nobel Prize for Literature.

I made this book required reading every year for my American History students in grade twelve. I also showed them the movie starring Henry Fonda. I wanted my students to see how ordinary everyday lives were devastated by the impact of the Great Depression.

One year, while showing the movie, some students snickered and giggled at the scene where the Joad family had to stop at the side of the road and bury their grandfather in an unmarked grave. I felt the need to say something to let them know their behaviour was inappropriate.

I shut the projector off, walked in the dark to the front of the room, and turned on only the lights that illuminate the blackboard. Then I turned to the class and said:

> Some of you thought that scene we have just seen was humorous. The only reason you were capable of that response is because you and your family have never lost your home and been forced to pile all your possessions into an old truck and drive thousands of miles in search of work — and on the way there, a member of your family dies, and without any money for a proper burial, a member of your family has to be buried at the side of the

highway in an unmarked grave. Nothing like that has ever happened to you — and I hope it never does.

Then I turned off the lights, walked to the back of the room, and turned on the projector again. The class watched the rest of the movie in respectful silence.

One year, one of my students, John Burry, recited Henry Fonda's "I'll Be There" speech from memory, the speech that Tom Joad said to his mother before he was forced to leave the family, probably for good. His mother knew at the time that she would probably never see her son again. John Burry could recite that speech to the class with a perfect imitation of Henry Fonda's voice. That brought history alive.

Thank you, John. I hope you're reading this. I'll never forget you for doing that.

Here is what Tom Joad said to his mother:

> "Well, maybe like Casy says, a fella ain't got a soul of his own, but on'y a piece of a big one — an' then — "
> "Then what, Tom?" said his mother.
> "Then it don' matter. Then I'll be all aroun' in the dark. I'll be everywhere —wherever you look. Wherever they's a fight so hungry people can eat, I'll be there. Wherever they's a cop beatin' up a guy, I'll be there. If Casy knowed, why, I'll be in the way guys yell when they're mad an' — I'll be in the way kids laugh when they're hungry an' they know supper's ready. An' when our folks eat the stuff they raise an' live in the houses they build — why, I'll be there …"

I told my students the book was very controversial when it was first published. Now it stands as the ultimate American classic. The ending did not appear in the movie, over the objections of Steinbeck.

The director, John Ford, did not think theatre audiences could handle it. Steinbeck's first publisher also wanted it left out so he found another publisher with enough courage to put it in. The stage play we saw in

Stratford included the ending. I referred to the ending before my students started reading the book. I did not describe what happened on the last page. I simply said this:

"When you get to the last page of this book, you will find that the Joad family is left with nothing. And I mean nothing. But even though they had nothing, they still found something they were willing to share with a total stranger. In many ways, the book is very sad, but it also portrays a triumph of the human spirit."

46

Did Columbus Really "Discover" America?

In October 1992, a TV crew from one of Toronto's stations arrived in my classroom at North Toronto Collegiate to see how I portrayed the arrival of Christopher Columbus in the New World in 1492. This month was the five-hundredth anniversary of that epic voyage, and many people were questioning the use of the word "discovered" when thousands of Native peoples had already been living in that part of the world for thousands of years.

I thoroughly enjoyed the teaching of this topic because of the drama of the first voyage taken by Columbus across the Atlantic. He was Italian, yet persuaded Queen Isabella of Spain to hock her jewels to pay for three ships in which he planned to sail west in order to reach the Far East. Those three ships, as every school child should know, were the *Nina*, the *Pinta*, and the *Santa Maria*.

Columbus apparently miscalculated the size of the Earth and thought it was much smaller than it actually is. When he found land, he found it where he expected to find it, and to his dying day believed that he had reached the outer islands of Asia. If he had known how big the world really was, he might never have sailed. But he did sail, and for decades the history books said he discovered America.

And that word "discover" brought the TV crew to my classroom. How, they wanted to know, did I handle the claim of "discovery"? Very simple, I said, while standing at the front of the class with my students seated. The use of the word "discover" is from the European point of view because for those people, this was a new discovery. From the viewpoint of the Native peoples already living there, they had discovered it much earlier.

I always mentioned, while talking about Columbus, a bumper sticker you sometimes see on cars in the United States: "AMERICA — A GOOD OLD ITALIAN NAME." And indeed it is, thanks to Martin Waldseemüller, a German cartographer who produced a map of the New World in 1507 based on the writings of Amerigo Vespucci, a Florentine navigator who sailed to the New World four times soon after Columbus "discovered" it. Waldseemüller labelled the new lands "America" from Vespucci's first name. If he had chosen his last name, the nation to the south of us would be called the United States of Vespuccia and its citizens would call themselves Vespuccians!

47

Guidance Report by Air Mail

I remember the day when I sent a guidance report to the vice-principal's office by air mail. This took place a few years after I began teaching at North Toronto Collegiate.

It was about two minutes after 9:00 a.m. and I had just started teaching my first-period class in Room 313 when the phone rang. It was Ron Kendall calling from the VP's office, asking for the guidance report that I was to fill out on behalf of one of my students and return it to the office the next day. Ron said he needed it right away because the parents of this student were sitting in his office at that very moment.

"I already have it filled out," I said. "But my class has just started and I don't want to send the report with a student to the office because the information is confidential. How should I get it to you?"

Ron replied, "Your class is on the same side of the building as my office. Fold it into a paper dart and throw it out the window. I'll catch it as it comes down!"

I folded the report as instructed, leaned out my window, took aim, and fired it off in the direction of Ron's first-floor office window. I watched as it slowly descended and landed in a bush outside Ron's window. It was too far out for him to reach out and retrieve it.

I excused myself from my class, ran downstairs, picked it out of the bush, and tried to throw it in through Ron's window. I could see him inside his office, waiting to catch it.

At first, it hit the wooden board designed to cut draughts and fell back onto the bush. I had to jump up and down several times in my attempt to send it inside. Every time I jumped up, I could see a serious-looking man and woman sitting at Mr. Kendall's desk and staring at me in disbelief. Mr. Kendall said to them, "That man you see jumping up and down outside my window is Mr. Sherk, your son's history teacher." He delivered that sentence in a very matter-of-fact way, as if to suggest that this sort of thing was a perfectly normal way of delivering reports to the office.

I finally got the report to go in through the window. Mr. Kendall smiled and waved at me as he unfolded the report, then I dashed back up three flights of stairs to return to my class. Mission accomplished! Certainly, it would have been easier to just walk it down in the first place, but this way was far more fun.

I have no idea what this full-size replica of a jersey cow was doing in the principal's office at North Toronto Collegiate, but Vice-Principal Ron Kendall and I could not resist having our picture taken with it.

48

Robert E. Lee to Lee Iacocca

Many years ago, the Audiovisual Department of the Toronto Board of Education purchased the entire thirteen-week made-for-TV *America* series narrated by British host Alistair Cook and covering almost the entire sweep of the American History course I was teaching at North Toronto Collegiate.

Thanks to that series, I learned for the first time that President Abraham Lincoln, at the outset of the American Civil War, offered the command of the Union Army to Robert E. Lee of Virginia. It was the most agonizing decision Lee ever had to face, and he spent all one day and all one night pacing back and forth in his upstairs bedroom before choosing to side with the South.

He said his family had lived in Virginia for five generations, and with that state opting to leave the Union and join the Confederacy, he felt he had no choice but to side with the South. He also added, perhaps as an attempt at self-justification, that any country held together by force of arms held no charm for him.

It was a tragic decision that probably doubled the length of the war. He was widely regarded — both then and now — as one of the most brilliant military leaders of all time. At the same time, he was regarded as a very compassionate man, and Alistair Cook remarked that it was odd he chose the profession of soldiering.

Later on in the American History course, we studied the rapid growth of American business in the decades following the Second World War, and especially how the Big Three (GM, Ford, and Chrysler) dominated the U.S. auto market in the 1950s and 1960s. We looked at the career of Lee Iacocca when he was at Ford and later at Chrysler, where, as its president, he successfully negotiated a ten-year loan from Washington to keep the company afloat (sound familiar?). I was driving through northern Michigan in the summer of 1983 when Iacocca came on the car radio to announce that the loan had been paid off in full seven years ahead of schedule: "It sure feels good to be out of hock!" he proudly proclaimed.

I always enjoyed showing my students the many connections between the past and the present, and Iacocca's career gave me another opportunity to do that. He was a rising star in the Ford Motor Company in 1956, working out of Philadelphia. His supervisor (a man named Charlie) liked Iacocca's enthusiasm, and picked him to travel through the southern states to all the Ford dealers to promote their new line of cars and trucks.

"But before I send you down there," said Charlie, as the story goes, "we have to do something about your name. If we introduce you as Mr. Iacocca, they'll think that's a foreign-sounding name and they might not warm up to you. So, for the purpose of this promotion, your first name will be your last name and your last name will be your first."

And so, over ninety years after the end of the American Civil War, Lee Iacocca travelled all through the southern states, and wherever he went, he was introduced as Mr. Iacocca Lee, creating the impression that he might be a direct descendant of that illustrious Confederate hero, Robert E. Lee.

And his first name (Iacocca)? Most people probably figured that was one of those funny-sounding names from the Bible. I learned that story about Lee Iacocca by reading his autobiography. And that's one of the reasons I loved teaching history. I was always learning new things.

Andy Lockhart, my history professor at the Ontario College of Education, gave us some good advice: "People your history." In other words, sprinkle your lessons with anecdotes about people and the unforgettable things they did.

49

Interview Your Grandparents

One of my favourite assignments for the grade ten Canadian History students was the essay based on an interview with their grandparents. Many of their grandparents had lived through the Great Depression and had many stories to tell.

And there was another benefit, as well. Each year, some students would thank me for giving them this assignment because they had never really talked to their grandparents before in detail about life when they were young — and this assignment often brought grandparents and grandchildren closer together.

Some grandparents talked about "collar and cuff" kits that you could buy at their neighbourhood store to replace the collar and cuffs on a shirt – thereby doubling the lifespan of the shirt.

Others mentioned how they could not afford to eat in restaurants, and their friends were in the same bind. They would often get together at each other's places and play cards for the evening. One grandmother said that people were closer together back then, and helped each other because everyone was feeling the impact of the Depression.

One grandfather, who was a young boy in the mid-1930s, remembers a man sitting in their kitchen and telling this boy's parents that he had lost his job and did not know how he was going to look after his family. For the first time in his life, that young boy saw a grown man cry.

For some students, their grandparents had either moved away or had passed away. For those students, I asked them to find someone in their neighbourhood who would be the approximate age of their grandparents, and interview those people. Here again was another benefit of this assignment. Some neighbourhood seniors were given the opportunity to talk about life when they were young. All too often, our seniors are ignored and neglected, yet they are an invaluable source of history because they actually lived through it.

Some of my students read their assignments out loud in class so all of us could benefit from the assignment. I was the last one to talk — and told the class about my maternal grandmother. She was born in Chatham, Ontario, in 1882 and was twenty-one years old before the Wright brothers flew their first airplane at Kitty Hawk in North Carolina in 1903. In other words, for the first twenty years of my grandmother's life, there were no airplanes anywhere because none had yet been built.

She lived long enough to see Neil Armstrong set foot on the moon on July 20, 1969. From the first flight at Kitty Hawk to the first footprint on the moon, that all happened in her lifetime. She died in Toronto on March 10, 1971, in her eighty-ninth year.

50
Three Students "Moon" a School Assembly

Streaking was a popular fad in the 1970s (see Chapter 26). By the 1980s, when I was teaching at North Toronto Collegiate, "mooning" had become a popular way of gaining attention. Newspapers regularly reported stories of individuals who pulled down their pants in public and showed their bare behind to the world. We never thought any of our students would do this, but three of them did. And they did it right in the middle of a school assembly with hundreds of students watching.

Ron Kendall, a vice-principal, was the master of ceremonies at this particular assembly. He stood at a podium with a microphone on one side of the stage. The curtains were drawn across the stage.

Suddenly, and without warning, three young men wearing masks (at least we think they were young men) stepped out from behind the curtains and onto centre stage, pulled their pants down in unison and "mooned" the entire school. Then they quickly pulled up their pants and disappeared. Some teachers chased after them, but could not catch them. The whole assembly was in an uproar with students talking excitedly to one another over what they had just witnessed.

It was up to Mr. Kendall to restore order after this interruption. He stepped up to the microphone again and I was wondering what he was going to say.

He said, "Ladies and gentlemen! You saw them and I saw them! And what you saw is what they are!"

A mighty cheer went up from the students for the way Mr. Kendall restored order with just a few well-chosen words, and the assembly proceeded as planned without further interruption.

51
Rock Around the Block!

In the spring of 1995, and with just two years to go before retirement, I drove to school in a car I had just purchased: a tomato-red 1947 Mercury convertible with a white top, red and white interior, and whitewall tires. It also had a radio and an electric *ah-OO-gah* horn, just like the ones on a Model A Ford.

Under the hood was a 350-cubic-inch Chevrolet V8 engine bolted to a 400 Turbo Automatic transmission. The car had been customized in the style popular when I was in high school in the 1950s. A previous owner, a man in Stoney Creek, Ontario, had done all the work. It was nosed (no hood ornament), decked (no handle or licence plate on the trunk lid), shaved (all door handles and side trim removed and holes filled in), molded (all four fenders blended to the body), and channelled (lowered). It looked like a car right out of *American Graffiti*.

On warm spring days, I would slide behind the wheel and, accompanied by other teachers, including Dennis Pascoe, Heather Cirulis, and Ian Waldron, we would put the top down, pull out of the teachers' parking lot, and drive around the block with the radio blaring all the big rock 'n' roll tunes from the 1950s and 1960s, including "Great Balls of Fire" by Jerry Lee Lewis, "Jailhouse Rock" by Elvis, "At the Hop" by Danny and the Juniors, "Chantilly Lace" by the Big Bopper, "Tutti Fruiti" by Little Richard, "School Days," by Chuck Berry, "Wake Up Little Susie" by the Everly Brothers, the odd song from the 1980s like "Wake Me Up Before You Go-Go" by Wham!, and of course, Bill Haley and the Comets belting out "Rock Around the Clock"!

Whenever that song came on, the whole carload of teachers in my '47 Merc ragtop would all join in and sing along, changing the words to "Rock Around the Block"!

The block consisted of a short stretch of Roehampton Avenue, which brought us heading west out onto Yonge Street, the main north-south street in Toronto, and one of the busiest. With a right turn onto Yonge, we threaded our way through the traffic until we reached the light at Broadway. Other drivers (and students too!) often smiled and often gave us a thumbs-up.

We hung a right at the light on Yonge and drove a full block along Broadway, alongside our school's football field, where students could be seen stretched out on the grass and eating their lunch. We always gave them a big *ah-OO-gah* with the horn and they waved back.

Then a short block down Redpath and back to Roehampton, which brought us back to the school parking lot. As many as five teachers were in the car (seat belts for five), and when we reached the parking lot, someone would ask: "Can we go around again?" And everyone in the car would shout "YES!"

Our lunch hour lasted seventy minutes and we took full advantage of the time, often eating in the car as we circled the block. And we always made it back to class on time.

One day in the hallway, a student I didn't teach said hello and said he had heard I had a really cool car. "Oh, have you been out to the parking lot to look at it?" I asked.

After seeing their teachers riding around the block at noon hour in my '47 Mercury convertible, I treated several students to a ride around the school parking lot (top down, of course).

"No," he said, "I haven't seen it yet, but I heard you blowing the horn while you were driving around the block."

To me, this photo is worth a million dollars. Dennis Pascoe was a fellow teacher at North Toronto Collegiate and we became very good friends. He always rode with me around the block at lunchtime in my 1947 Mercury convertible. His retirement was sadly short-lived. He died of leukemia.

52
A Most Unusual Question

Mike Frayn was a student in one of my grade ten Canadian history classes at North Toronto Collegiate. He sat at the front of the second row in from the door and sometimes asked questions directly to me while the class was working at their desks on an assignment.

It was a very good and enthusiastic class and none of the students caused any problems. This was partly owing to the credit system in which every student had an individual timetable, and whenever the bell rang, they scattered in different directions to take whatever subject was next on their timetable. They would be sitting with some of the same students and some different ones every time they changed classes. When this particular class came together in my class, they were all eager to learn. I was lucky to have them. Not every class was like this.

Well, one day Mike Frayn asked me a question. It was a question I had never heard before and never heard it again:

"Mr. Sherk, how come you never get mad at us like all our other teachers do?"

"Well, Mike," I said, "this class has never done anything to make me mad."

He hesitated before saying, "Do you suppose you could get mad at us just to show us what you're like when you're mad?"

I began pounding my fist on my desk and raised my voice: "Mike Frayn! Don't you ever ask me a question like that ever again! Not ever! And if you do, I will send you to the office and recommend that you be expelled from this school!"

Mike smiled and said, "Thank you, Mr. Sherk."

53

Voting on Date and Format of Test

The one compulsory history course in Ontario high schools is the one usually offered in grade ten: Canadian History from 1896 to the present day. It starts at 1896 with the election of Wilfrid Laurier as Canada's first French-Canadian prime minister, and his arrival in office ushered in a spectacular growth in Canada's population, with immigrants streaming in and filling up the West.

This course also included a special unit on government called Civics, in which the students learned about our federal system of government and how it operates. We would examine all the parts of our political system and how they interact with each other. I often compared the different parts of our government to the parts of a car. All the parts have been designed to operate together so that the car — and country — can function.

One of the best ideas I ever heard for teaching the role of political parties and the running of elections came from Kerry Keenan, a fellow history teacher at North Toronto Collegiate. Here is how it worked:

Near the end of the unit on government, I would announce an upcoming test to cover the unit. The students could vote on what kind of test they wanted. Here were the options:

Test on Friday — fill in the blanks

Test on Friday — essay-style questions

Test on Friday — combination of blanks and essay

Test on Monday — fill in the blanks

Test on Monday — essay style questions

Test on Monday — combination of blanks and essay

I then announced the formation of political parties so that the students could get together who wanted the same kind of test and then try to persuade the whole class to vote in favour of that. Here were the names of the parties:

FRI-BLANK
FRI-ESS
FRI-COM
MON-BLANK
MON-ESS
MON-COM

The party name revealed what it stood for. Then I designated certain areas of the classroom where like-minded people could meet to form a political party:

"The FRI-BLANK party will meet in the southeast corner … the FRI-ESS party in the northeast corner … the FRI-COM in the northwest corner … the MON-BLANK in the southwest corner … the MON-ESS in the centre of the room … and the MON-COM party out in the hall!"

On a given signal, I would tell the students to head to that part of the room that represents the kind of test they want to have. The thirty or so students in the class then got up out of their desks and headed in all directions. Usually, every position had some supporters and six political parties would emerge, some larger than others.

Next announcement: "Now get together with your other party members and elect a leader!"

This would take about a minute or two.

Next announcement: "Now help your party leader prepare a speech which he or she will deliver to the entire class to try to get everyone to vote in favour of what this party wants."

This would take another few minutes.

I would then ask each party to write its party name on a slip of paper and place it in a basket. I would then ask a student to close his or her eyes and pull the slips of paper out of the basket, one after the other. This will determine the order of speeches.

Then each party leader would get up and deliver a speech, urging everyone to vote for their party and giving reasons why they should. The parties that favoured a Friday test usually said the material would be fresh in their minds for having studied it in class all week, and besides, a Monday test would ruin the weekend. Better to get it over with on Friday. The parties that favoured Monday usually said that the weekend would provide extra time to prepare for it and would probably result in a better mark.

The format of the test was also an issue. The ones who favoured blanks said the test can be done faster. The ones who favoured essay-style questions argued that those questions are better training for the final exam. And some favoured a combination of the two.

During the speeches, occasionally a student would abandon his or her party and switch to another, but the party ranks usually held firm.

Then the entire class would vote by secret ballot.

Almost always, with six political parties, no one achieved a majority. I would then appoint myself as governor general and go out into hallway to talk to the party leaders. I would ask, "Who is able to compromise and work together with one of the other parties in order to form the government?"

The number of votes they received represented the number of seats they won in the House of Commons. Usually two parties would come together with some kind of compromised plan in order to form a government. Sometimes the test would be split with half given on Friday and the other half on Monday.

By going through this process, the students gained a much better understanding of the role of political parties in our political system. And I always enjoyed pointing out to them that the British North America Act makes no mention of political parties. They arose simply because people with similar political views got together.

54
"You're Giving Me a Zero?"

While I stayed home one day with the twenty-four-hour flu, a supply teacher covered my classes and gave the assignments I left for him. He collected them from each class and left a note on top of the pile, instructing me that one of my students had misbehaved and therefore should be given a mark of zero.

That student was one of my best students and I was surprised that he presented a problem for the supply teacher. However, I had to take some kind of action to satisfy the supply teacher, or he might never fill in for me again. The student, on the other hand, might claim that he did nothing wrong and I was not there to see what had actually happened.

I took the student aside right after class and showed him the note. I could tell by the look on his face that he was ready to dispute it. Before he could get any words out, I said, "I cannot ignore a note like this. However, you have always been a good student in my class and so I will enter a mark of zero in pencil, and as long as no supply teacher leaves a note like this again with your name on it, I will erase the zero at the end of the term and give you the good mark I'm sure you deserve."

He thought that was fair and the matter never came up again.

55

"I Hear You're Writing a Screenplay!"

While I was teaching at North Toronto Collegiate, most of my classes during those twenty-one years were held in Room 304 on the southeast corner of the building. Ken Olsen taught English in Room 305 right next door, and one of the courses he taught was a media course to his OAC English students, when Ontario schools still had that thirteenth grade.

He heard that a friend of mine named Derf Teews (a.k.a. Dr. Fred Sweet) and I were attempting to write a screenplay for an original full-length feature film that we were hoping would be released in motion picture theatres all over North America just as soon as we could finish writing it. Mr. Olsen asked if I would come into his class and talk about the business of writing a screenplay. How were we going about it? How were we developing a story? How were we moving it from scene to scene? How were we developing the characters? Where and when was the action taking place? How were we building everything up to a climax? What gave us the idea to tackle this project in the first place? And ... the question near and dear to my heart ... how does the movie begin?

The students were eager to hear every word I had to say. For most of them, this was the first time they had had any exposure to someone who might be writing a screenplay, and some probably felt that Hollywood was just around the corner.

"Well," I began, "let me describe the opening scene, and then we'll go from there. Imagine if you will, a car like the car that James Dean drove in *Rebel Without a Cause* (some of the students had actually seen that movie, even though it was made in 1954). It was a black and sinister-looking 1949 Mercury two-door coupe with fender skirts and Hollywood mufflers and big wide 'gangster' whitewalls. Now imagine that same car as a convertible and the top is down. It's sitting in the middle of a gravel road between endless fields of ripe tomatoes, apparently having broken down while being driven. The driver is trying to get it started. And the camera filming this scene is behind and slightly above the car. Each time the driver turns the key to try and start the car (*r-r-r-r-r-r*), the camera moves closer to the rear bumper, where we see a black-and-white 1957 Ontario licence plate. When the driver stops trying to start the car, the camera stops. When he tries again, the camera moves closer. Each time the engine turns over, the camera moves closer to the rear of the car … *r-r-r-r-r-r* … *r-r-r-r-r-r* …. *r-r-r-r-r-r* … two chrome tailpipes are sticking out at the back of the car. The camera approaches one of the tailpipes … *r-r-r-r-r-r* … and enters it.

"Now the camera is travelling through the tailpipe as the driver continues trying to start the car. It moves through the muffler (*r-r-r-r-r-r* …), it moves through the exhaust pipe (*r-r-r-r-r-r* …), it enters the combustion chamber and stops just inches from the piston coming up to the spark plug.

"At that precise instant, a spark jumps across the gap in the spark plug and a HUGE FIREBALL EXPLOSION fills the entire screen. The car has started with a mighty roar, blowing the camera right out of the exhaust system and back onto the gravel road.

"The driver pulls into first gear, rams his foot to the floor, and speeds away with gravel spraying all over the camera lens."

Then I stood there in front of the class, looking at them staring at me and waiting eagerly for me to continue.

I said nothing. I just stood there. Finally, a student said, "Well, Mr. Sherk, don't leave us hanging! What happens next?"

I don't remember exactly what I said next because the storyline has changed several times since that day in Mr. Olsen's class. I do recall saying that the writing of fiction (and this was to be an original story) poses challenges never faced by writers of non-fiction. When you write non-fiction, you are writing about things that have actually happened. That is your raw material and you work with it.

"When you are writing fiction," I said, "anything goes. Or does it? The storyline, however far-fetched, has to make sense on some level or no one will read it or (in the case of a movie that goes nowhere), no one will want to watch it. And the dialogue? You have to make up the words that your fictitious characters are speaking in order to reveal what they are about, and to advance the plot.

"Like non-fiction, your original story probably has a time and a place where the action unfolds. You have to decide on a number of things. In what year or years does your story take place? Is it all on one day or across several years? Is it in one locale or several? How will you tie all the pieces together? What names will you give to your characters? How many characters will you have? Does your background prepare you in any way for tackling this project? Are any parts semi-autobiographical?

"In screen-writing, generally one page of print equals one minute on the screen. If you are aiming for a movie of one-and-a-half hours, your screenplay should run to about ninety or one hundred pages. You should be able to sum up your story in a paragraph of fifty words or less. And you have to ask: 'What is your title?'"

"And what is the title of *your* screenplay, Mr. Sherk?" asked one of the students.

"We've gone through several titles," I replied. "It's best not to get too hung up on this part because the final title might not come to you until you have finished the story. It helps to have a working title simply to identify the project you are working on."

"And what is your working title at the present time, Mr. Sherk?"

"Well," I replied, "before this movie is made, it might have to come out as a book first. And if the book is a bestseller, that increases its chances of hitting the big screen. All I can give you is the working title of the book."

Long pause. "The title of the book? *I Can't Wait To See The Movie!*"

If any of those students I spoke to over fifteen years ago are reading this book, I am pleased to report that I am still working on the story.

56

History Jokes I Told in Class

If you tell a joke in class, you can never be sure if it will get a big laugh. Teenagers can be unpredictable, and a joke that adults think is funny may fall on deaf ears when told to your students. To protect myself from telling a joke that might go over like the proverbial "lead balloon," I prefaced the joke by saying, "I'm going to tell you a joke that history teachers think is hilarious. If you don't laugh, that's okay, but history teachers think it's really funny."

I would pause for a few seconds and say nothing. I could always count on one or more students to say: "Well, what are you waiting for, Mr. Sherk? Tell us the joke!"

I told them about the monk who joined a monastery and had to take a vow of silence. He could speak only two words once every seven years. He prayed every day and read the Bible and worked in the fields. The years rolled by.

Finally, after seven years, the abbot called the monk into his office and said, "Young man, you have been here seven years in total silence. You may now say two words. What might those two words be?"

"Too cold," replied the monk.

"Well," said the abbot, "we've had similar complaints from other monks. We'll try to hang some extra animal skins over the open windows on the north side, and that may help. Now back to your prayers."

The next seven years rolled by and the abbot called the monk back into his office. "You may now say two more words. What two words would you like to say?"

"Food rotten," said the monk.

"Ah," said the abbot. "A familiar complaint from the other monks, as well. I'll speak to the cook and we'll see what we can do."

Another seven years rolled by. The abbot called the monk into his office again and asked what two words he would like to say now.

"I quit!" said the monk.

"Well, I'm glad to hear that," said the abbot, "because you have done nothing but complain ever since you came here twenty-one years ago."

Every class has its own distinct personality. Some classes laughed, some smiled, and some did neither. I got the biggest laughs when I told this joke to a group of adults.

57

Alexander the Great Died of a Fever...

Around the end of September every year, we held what we called "Mini-Night," at which the parents of our students could follow their timetable through a typical day and meet all their teachers, who would have eight minutes to explain the course for their subject. Then the bell would ring and they would rush off to the next class.

The line that always got a laugh from the parents (and you really had to be there to appreciate the humour) was in my description of the grade eleven Ancient and Medieval History course. It began in prehistoric times, followed by the emergence of cities (and civilization) in the Middle East and Egypt. We took them through the building of the pyramids, the rise and fall of the Babylonians, the sea voyages of the Phoenicians with their ships built from the cedars of Lebanon, the development of writing, the early days of ancient Greece with the writings of Homer, the Minoan civilization on the island of Crete, the rise of city-states on the Greek mainland (especially Athens and Sparta), the wars with Persia followed by the Peloponnesian War, and then the rise of Alexander the Great, who came down from Macedon, conquered Greece, and then used it as a springboard to invade the mighty Persia Empire.

All these details, and many more, had to be covered in the fall term to clear the deck for the rise of ancient Rome during the winter term. I conveyed a sense of urgency in moving forward through all these historical records, with each passing day bringing us closer and closer to the completion of the fall term.

"Every year," I intoned, "we have to maintain the correct pace so that Alexander the Great dies of a fever in Babylon just before the Christmas exams."

58

Wardrobe Changes in Thirty-One Years

I stood in front of my first classroom on Tuesday, September 6, 1966, and I still remember the names of some of the students in my grade ten home form class, including Gary Balaam and George Benedek, who both offered to take the attendance slip down to the office.

Anxious to make a good first impression, I wore a black three-piece suit with the jacket open to show off my vest. My black shoes were polished to a dazzling sheen. My tie had a tie clip and I think I even wore cuff links. By the end of the day, chalk dust adorned my black suit and, on the following day, I wore my only other suit, a dark green two-piece outfit. The black suit went to the local cleaners for a cleaning and pressing because I wanted the crease in my trousers to be razor-sharp. On the third day, I was back in class wearing my three-piece while the cleaners were pressing my green suit from the day before. And so it went all month, black, green, black, green, black, green …

On the last day of the month, I got quite a shock. My cleaning bill was threatening to gobble up all our grocery money! From then on, I had to be more realistic about cleaning and pressing. I still kept wearing just the black and green suits for the rest of the school year, but took them to the cleaners once a week instead of once a day.

Speaking of clothing, I was sitting in the staff room one day when the subject of student clothing came up. One older teacher turned to me and said, "Bill, this is your first year of teaching, and you have a lot of things to keep track of, but I certainly hope you are not allowing any of your students to come to class wearing jeans."

"What's the matter with students wearing jeans?" I asked, not having ever considered the question before.

"Jeans represent an undesirable attitude and should not be permitted in class," he said. "Have you permitted any of your students to come to class wearing jeans?"

"Well," I replied, "I'm so busy keeping my history lesson on track, the students could come to class wearing clown outfits and I wouldn't even notice. But I'll tell you what. I have a class starting in a few minutes and I'll check to see if any jeans walk in."

A few minutes later, the bell rang and I headed off to my grade eleven Ancient History class in Room 218 (I taught in fourteen rooms in my first year). After everyone got seated, I stared up and down each row, looking for the dreaded blue jeans. The students probably thought I was checking for litter on the floor and didn't say anything. Aha! Halfway down the centre row, a male student was sitting at his desk and wearing BLUE JEANS! His name was John Plaskett. He was a first-class honours student with marks in the nineties. And his mother was Ida Plaskett, the highly respected assistant head of the English Department at our school. That day was the one and only time I concerned myself with what the students wore to class. Now on with the lesson!

In June 1968, Pierre Trudeau became Prime Minister of Canada and popularized the turtleneck in place of a tie. By this time, my three-piece black suit was hanging in the closet at home, awaiting weddings and funerals, and my green suit had been replaced with a sport jacket and dress pants of non-matching colours (although I remember some teachers who thought they should wear a suit every day and would show up in a sport jacket and dress pants that were almost — but not quite — a perfect match.)

Thanks to our new prime minister, I said good-bye to my necktie and started wearing a turtleneck. Around this same time, designer jeans became popular and so my dress pants stayed in the closet and I sported the latest model of Jordache jeans (remember them?). The jeans worked wonders on the family budget because I could throw them into the washing machine every night! A tan corduroy jacket and a pair of cowboy boots completed the new look. The years rolled by and whenever my jeans and boots wore out, I'd buy replacements. Then in September 1984, my teaching wardrobe took another sudden turn in a new direction when I introduced the "Sherkout" to my students (see Chapter 39 for the full story). It was important for the students to see the different aerobic moves I was taking them through to the beat of the music, and so I climbed up onto my desk at the front of the room and had them stand in the aisle while we joined in chanting, "Window! Door! Ceiling! Floor!" as well as all the other wild and crazy gyrations that went with every Sherkout. Now I needed footwear with a good grip so I could do the Sherkouts on the top of my desk and so I said goodbye to my cowboy boots and bought a pair of white running shoes. And so, from top to bottom, my transformation was complete: shirt or sweater, light blue jeans, and white running shoes. That's the way I dressed for the last thirteen years of my teaching career and I loved it! But we didn't do a Sherkout every day. At the most, once a week. And so, every once in a while on a non-Sherkout day, I would put on my black three-piece suit and wear it to school for no particular reason. The reaction was incredible and very favourable — but would I be showered with compliments if I wore it every day? I think not.

Susie Horvath was a student in one of my history classes at North Toronto Collegiate Institute. Her parents operated Horvath Photography Studio near the school and I went there in 1988 to have my picture taken.

59

An Italian Motorcycle in My History Class

It was a warm day in spring and the last class of the day. It was my grade ten Canadian history class, and less than a month remained of the school year. We were at a part of the course that had to be covered in time for the final exam.

We were working on a chapter describing the work of Premier Jean Lesage in the early 1960s and the various reforms he introduced. First we talked about his pension reforms, not a topic close to the heart of teenagers. I could see by the glazed look in their eyes that I had to try harder than normal to hold their attention. Here's what I wrote on the blackboard:

PEN$ION REFORM$

I thought I was very clever in adding the dollar signs, and they copied all the letters down listlessly into their notes. I could tell they wanted to be anywhere except a history class.

The next reform was in the area of healthcare, again not a topic guaranteed to grab the attention of teenagers. I made a clumsy attempt to write the word HEALTH on the board in the form of a picture with the two *H*s as the head and foot of a hospital bed and with the other letters representing the patient. I hung an intravenous bag from the letter T. Again, they copied it down but very slowly, and some of them were yawning.

I was desperate. The lesson was sliding downhill and we still had fifteen minutes to go. I don't think even a Sherkout would have revived them. Then an idea!

"I want you all to look at me and tell me what kind of vehicle I am driving," I said, as I put my hands out in front of me, curved my fingers around some imaginary handlebars, and made the sound of an engine revving up.

Right away, they perked up. A kid from the back of the room shouted out the answer: "A motorcycle, SIR! You're riding a motorcycle!"

Just then, by sheer coincidence, a biker rode by the school with a thunderous blast from his mufflers. Things were starting to look up in Room 304.

Then I said, "Yes, I'm riding a motorcycle. But what brand is it?"

The boys in the class rose to the challenge. One of them said, "I'll bet it's an English bike. I can see Mr. Sherk riding an English motorcycle from the sixties."

"Yes," said another one. "And I'll bet it's a Royal Enfield."

"No, it isn't," I said.

"A Triumph?"

"No."

"A BSA?"

"No."

"A Matchless?"

"No."

"An Ariel?"

"No."

"An AJS?"

"No."

"Then it must be a Norton!" a student proudly proclaimed.

"No it isn't," I said.

Then someone asked if it was from England. I said "No."

"Then it's got to be a Harley!" someone said.

"No."

"A Honda!" someone shouted.

"No."

"A Suzuki!"

"No."

"A Kawasaki!"

"No. But I'll give you a hint. It's an Italian bike."

Dead silence for three seconds. Then a boy at the back of the room, who had never had his hand up before, began pumping his hand in the air and bouncing up and down in his seat; he was so excited!

"Is it a Ducati, Mr. Sherk?"

"Yes, it is, George. Please come to the front and write that name on the board in big capital letters for everyone to copy down." This he did:

DUCATI

After everyone copied it down, I stared at them for a few seconds, not saying anything. They were sitting on the edge of their seats, wondering what was coming next.

"A couple of minutes ago, we were talking about the reforms introduced by the Jean Lesage government in Quebec in the early sixties. Then all of a sudden we started talking about motorcycles. What's the connection?"

Dead silence. Then I said, "Look again on the page in your textbook we're working from. We've covered pension reforms and healthcare reforms and …"

My voice trailed off as they took a closer look at their textbooks.

Then a boy sitting over near the window stood up and proudly proclaimed: "Mr. Sherk, I know what the connection is. May I show you on the board?"

"Please do," I said.

He came to the front of the room and I handed him a piece of chalk. Before he wrote anything on the board, he spoke to the class as if he was training to be a history teacher: "Mr. Sherk has mentioned two reforms of the Jean Lesage government in Quebec in the early sixties: pension reform and healthcare reform. But that's not all. A third reform is mentioned in our textbook and that is why the name of a motorcycle is on the blackboard."

The other students looked at him in stunned amazement as he turned to the board and added a letter at the front of Ducati:

EDUCATI

Then he went to the other end of the word and added two more letters:

EDUCATION

"The third great reform," the student at the front said with visible pride, "introduced by the Jean Lesage government in Quebec in the early Sixties was in the field of … EDUCATION!"

"That's right!" I shouted as I led the class in a big round of applause.

Just after the applause died down, I heard a boy at the front of the room lean over and whisper something to his friend across the aisle:

"That's the coolest thing I've ever seen."

60

High School Reunion in 1966

It was the spring of 1996 and I was one year away from retirement when I heard of an upcoming high school reunion. The Leamington District Secondary School was planning to celebrate its 100th anniversary. The school itself was built in 1953, replacing an older high school across the street which was built in 1923. That one replaced the original Leamington high school, which opened its doors in 1896 in a Victorian mansion formerly owned by Leamington's Member of Parliament, Lewis Wigle. He donated his house to the school board.

I heard about the reunion from some friends in Leamington, who phoned me in Toronto to tell me about it. Then I phoned the high school in Leamington and asked to be put on their mailing list. The receptionist asked me what years I had attended. I told her I never went to the Leamington high school but I had attended Selkirk Public school in Leamington and knew a lot of the students who attended the high school.

"I'm sorry, Sir," she replied. "I am only authorized to send out reunion information to former students of this high school."

I tried another tack. "Well," I said, "I bought my first car from one of the janitors at the high school. His name was Cliff Garant. He left the car parked in the mud behind the football field and that's where I picked it up. It had no engine and I had to push it home."

"Well, that's different," the receptionist said. "You have a legitimate connection to this high school and I will be happy to add your name to our mailing list."

The information arrived and I made plans to attend in July, when lots of people were on vacation and many former students who had moved away planned their holidays to coincide with the reunion.

I had attended Selkirk Public School in Leamington from 1952 to 1954 for grades five, six, and seven, following our family's move from

Toronto to Leamington. Beginning in September 1954, I attended UTS in Toronto, a school my older brother John began attending the year before. During our high school years, we lived at our Toronto home during each school year and spent our summers at our home in Leamington. That way, we could keep in touch with many of the people we knew from attending public school in Leamington.

The day arrived for me to slide behind the wheel and drive from Toronto to Leamington for the high school reunion. The car I owned at the time was a street rodded 1947 Mercury convertible with personalized "SHERK" license plates. The car was known as the "Sherk Merc" and was tomato red, a very appropriate colour for Leamington, the Tomato Capital of Canada.

My trip was relatively uneventful until I turned off Hwy. 401, drove south on Hwy. 4, and headed west on Hwy. 3, with ninety miles to go to Leamington. I was on Hwy. 3 for only about ten miles when I looked in my rear view mirror and saw a gang of bikers on their motorcycles about half a mile behind me. This stretch of highway was relatively deserted, and I wondered if they were friendly. The car I was driving would certainly attract their attention and I would be outnumbered.

My 1947 "Sherk Merc."

Wallacetown was just up ahead and so I pulled into their one and only gas station, figuring the bikers would keep on going and I could resume my trip without worrying about anything.

To my surprise, the bikers also pulled in and stopped at that same gas station.

One of them, in a black leather jacket, dismounted and walked over to my car.

"I see the name 'SHERK' on your license plate," he said. "Are you by any chance the Bill Sherk who knew Peter Clancy at UTS in Toronto?"

"Why, yes, I am," I replied. Peter Clancy had been one year behind me at UTS, which I attended from 1954 to 1961 (from grade seven to grade thirteen). Peter and I had become good friends in high school and we shared a passion for old cars. I owned a 1940 Mercury convertible with a '283' Chev V-8 under the hood (the same car I picked up from the mud behind the Leamington high school) and Peter owned a 1939 Mercury convertible with an Olds Rocket V-8 engine under his hood. Peter tragically was killed in a motorcycle accident in Port Credit in June 1964.

"How did you know Peter Clancy?" I asked the biker. "And what is your name?"

Extending his hand, he said, "I'm Doug Wood. I was a classmate of Peter's at UTS and knew that he and you were friends."

"Well," I replied. "What I'm going to tell you is almost unbelievable. I'm on my way to Leamington to a reunion at a high school I did not go to, and on the way there, I now meet someone who went to the high school I went to in Toronto. What would be the chances of this happening? A million to one?"

Doug and I reminisced for a few minutes about our old high school, which incidentally celebrated its 100th anniversary in the spring of 2010. Then he told me that he and his biker friends were on a camping excursion through southwestern Ontario.

"But we've never been this way before," he said. "Do you know of any restaurants up the road where we could stop for lunch?"

"Blenheim is about thirty miles from here and you'll find several restaurants right on the main street," I said.

"That sounds great," said Doug. "And since you're familiar with this area and going the same way we are, how would it be if you lead us there?

We'll get into formation right behind this cool car of yours and follow you right down the highway."

And so we did. I'm now driving along Hwy. 3 feeling like the King of the Road as I led about thirty bikers on their motorcycles for thirty miles to Blenheim, where they followed me right down the main street. I parked, they parked, and they thanked me. They invited me to join them for lunch but I was expected in Leamington for lunch and had to go.

As I pulled away, I waved at Doug Wood and his friends and reflected upon the many surprising twists and turns on the highway of life.

61
Reciting the Alphabet Backwards

As a teacher, I was always looking for new and unusual ways to introduce a new topic or chapter in my history classes. I tried the following approach in a grade ten Canadian history class about halfway through the school year.

"Can anyone in this class recite the alphabet backwards from *Z* to *A* without making a mistake? Who would like to try? There's a bonus mark for everyone who makes the attempt, and TWO bonus marks for the first student who does it right."

Several hands went into the air, eager to tackle this latest learning challenge.

"Now, before we begin, there is something I have to tell you. As you recite it, the rest of us will be listening carefully and watching for a mistake. And if you make a mistake, we will start pounding on our desks, just like they do in the House of Commons in Ottawa. And that will be your signal to sit down."

Well, the first three that tried it fumbled the ball somewhere between *Q* and *P* (it's important to watch your *P*s and *Q*s, whether forwards or backwards). Then a fourth student offered to try.

This was a young man who was very quiet in class and I suppose very shy. I was surprised to see him volunteer, but I was happy that he did because this would be a chance for him to get more involved in our lessons.

He stood up, smiled, then rhymed off all the letters in perfect order without any hesitation. He could actually recite the alphabet backwards as fast as the rest of us could recite it forwards. When he finished, he received a thunderous round of applause, then a standing ovation. From then on, he was no longer shy and quiet.

Now, you might wonder what was the purpose of starting a lesson in this very unorthodox manner. I told the class, "Whenever the alphabet is recited backwards, the letter at the end is … and on the count of three … I want all of you to shout in unison to tell me what that letter is. Okay, now … ONE … TWO … THREE!"

"*A!*" they shouted.

"Louder!" I yelled.

"*A!*" they shouted again.

"Louder!" I yelled.

Now they really put their heart into it:

"*A!*" they screamed.

"Thank, you," I said. "Now, what is the first letter of the first word in the first sentence on page 165 of your textbook?"

They flipped open their textbooks and every hand went into the air.

"Now tell me what it is."

They all screamed "*A*" again.

"And why is it *A?*" I asked.

"Because, Mr. Sherk," one of the students said, "it starts a chapter dealing with Al Capone, the Chicago gangster."

"That's right. But what is the title of our textbook?"

An answer came back: "*Spotlight Canada.*"

"That's right. A Canadian history textbook, and yet an entire chapter in this book is devoted to a Chicago gangster who maybe never even set foot in Canada. What's going on here?"

That started our study of Prohibition in Canada and the United States. South of the border, you were not allowed by law to drink it or manufacture alcohol. Here in Canada we were not supposed to drink it, but we could still manufacture it for export. And gangsters like Al Capone eagerly transported Canadian booze into the U.S. for thirsty Americans.

We spent about a week on the topic, which included the Kevin Costner movie, *The Untouchables*. At the end of this unit, Al Capone was being shipped off to Alcatraz to serve a prison term for tax evasion.

Many years ago on television, a series called *The Untouchables* was narrated by the famous American newscaster, Walter Winchell. The series followed Capone's career from start to finish, right up to the day he was brought into Alcatraz.

I loved dramatizing to the class what happened on the day Capone got to Alcatraz. I got this straight from the TV series, and whether it was historically accurate or not, I don't know. But it was a great way to finish the unit.

I had two students volunteer to play two roles at the front of the room. The one seated at my desk was the clerk checking Al Capone into Alcatraz. And the one standing beside my desk was Capone himself. Here is what was said:

Clerk: "Well, I guess you're next. What's your name?"

Capone: (with arrogant swagger) "Whaddaya mean 'What's my name?' Everybody knows my name!"

Clerk: "Well, if everybody knows your name, then you must know it, too. So what is it?"

Capone: (with barely supressed anger) "Capone."

Clerk: "How do you spell it?"

Capone: (another long pause while restraining his temper) "C-A-P-O-N-E."

Clerk: "And what's your first name?"

Capone: (looking resigned and defeated) "Al."

The bigger they are, the harder they fall.

62

How the Future Became the Past

When I began teaching in September 1966, I could draw upon five thousand years of recorded history for my lesson plans. I knew I would never run out of material, and I never did. But what I didn't think of at the beginning of my career was how the flow of history would shape my lessons over the ensuing years.

Take Quebec, for example. A chapter in the grade ten history textbook took us up to the government of Jean Lesage in the early 1960s. The October crisis with the FLQ was still four years in the future. The Parti Québécois, formed in 1968, would not win an election in Quebec for another eight years. And the first Quebec referendum was still fourteen years in the future. The second referendum was twenty-nine years ahead of us. Some of my students rode on a Unity Bus to Montreal in 1995. These students had not even been born when I first started teaching.

As time went by, I became very conscious of the fact that some of the material I was teaching was based on things that had happened during my years as a teacher, and I could say to my classes, "I remember when …" In other words, I was becoming an eyewitness to the flow of history.

I often referred to items in the newspaper to encourage my students to follow the daily news as history in the making. One day, I wrote the names of all three Toronto daily newspapers on the blackboard like this:

THE GLOBE AND MAIL
THE TORONTO STAR
THE TORONTO SUN

Then I would ask the class why the *Globe and Mail* was at the top and the *Toronto Sun* at the bottom, and the *Toronto Star* in the middle.

The usual answers would be that the *Globe and Mail* is the business paper and is aimed at a highly educated reading public whereas the *Toronto Sun* is mostly for sports and entertainment, with the *Toronto Star* being a mixture of the two.

"Could there be any other reason they are listed this way?" I would then ask.

Dead silence as they pondered the list again. Finally, a hand would shoot up and a student would proudly proclaim: "I know, SIR! I know."

"Tell us, please."

"You have listed the papers in alphabetical order!"

"Correct!"

63

When I Was in High School...

Looking back at my five years in high school (when we had grade thirteen), the things I remember most had nothing to do with what we were taught in class. One of my most memorable experiences took place the day I was kicked out of French class, even if only for a few minutes. Here is how it happened.

Soon after Elvis hit the top of the charts with "Heartbreak Hotel" and "Hound Dog," I decided I wanted to look like him and the quickest way would be to grow a pair of sideburns. But I wasn't old enough (I was only thirteen). And so I did the next best thing: I got a piece of charcoal and gave myself a pair of imitation sideburns.

I applied these in the boys' washroom at school because my mother would never let me leave the house looking like that. My new look was short-lived. My first class of the day was French with George Kirk. I was sitting at the back of the room, but even at that distance, Mr. Kirk could tell I looked different. He came down the aisle, opened his pocketknife as if to shave me, then said, "Sherk, go wash your face!"

64

No Smoking!

I never smoked as a teenager because I had no choice. Around the age of twelve, I discovered that I was allergic to several things, including feathers, mould, dust, and tobacco. Every week on the way home from school in Toronto, I stopped at a doctor's office for allergy shots. If I didn't get them, the things I was allergic to would make me cough ... and cough ... and cough ... Fortunately, my older brother and mother did not smoke, and my father only smoked cigars while in his car or in a designated room in the house.

And so, at a time when many teenagers began smoking, I opted not to take up the habit. I attended a high school in Toronto at Bloor and Spadina and the rule there was that you could not smoke within two blocks of the school. I remember walking south one lunch hour with three or four classmates when one of them lit up only a block from school. Just after he took his first puff, a big blue Oldsmobile screeched to a stop at the curb, the window came down, and the man behind the wheel barked, "Macfarlane, get in!" It was the headmaster! He drove around the block with John Macfarlane (future editor of *Toronto Life* magazine) a captive in his car while he lectured him on the rule of no smoking within two blocks of the school. He then deposited him back on the sidewalk where he had scooped him up a minute earlier. "What did he say?" we all wanted to know.

"He said it looks like hell," Macfarlane replied. "And if you think about it, it really does look like hell."

I heard that some of the teachers were known to smoke in their offices at school, but I never actually saw any of them doing it.

September of 1966 was my first month of teaching at Northern Secondary (my first month teaching anywhere). Toward the end of that month, I was requested to attend a meeting in the guidance office after school, where half a dozen other teachers had gathered to discuss something. The office was not large, and we were somewhat cramped in our seating. A couple of seats away, I saw a teacher light up a cigarette. This was the first time in my life I had ever seen a teacher smoking. I turned to the teacher sitting beside me and asked, "Is he allowed to smoke in here?"

He replied, "Welcome to the adult world."

I had not yet visited the staff room because my first-year timetable kept me constantly on the run, teaching in fourteen rooms all over the building, which housed 2,400 students and 140 teachers. About halfway through my first year, I finally found a few minutes to spare and dropped into the staff room. A bluish haze hung in the air as teacher after teacher puffed on cigarettes.

As the years rolled by, the hazards of smoking became more apparent, and the smoking issue for teachers became a hot item at staff meetings. The smokers offered to sit at just one end of the staff room to smoke while the non-smokers could sit at the other end. This suggestion was voted down on the grounds that you cannot have a peeing section at one end of a swimming pool.

When I finally retired in June 1997, no smoking by anyone (staff or students) was permitted anywhere on school property, and the few teachers who were still smoking by then had to do it on the other side of the street, or elsewhere.

65
Three Magic Words

Twice a year, Toronto high school students were given a day off to permit their teachers to participate in a Professional Development Day. Often a guest speaker in the morning spoke to a large number of teachers on a wide variety of topics — student motivation and evaluation, various teaching techniques, effective methods of chairing committee meetings, organizing music and sports programs, reading and writing and speaking skills, and so on.

One of the best speakers I ever heard was Father McGrath, a Roman Catholic priest from Boston who spoke to two thousand teachers at Massey Hall in downtown Toronto. With a microphone slung around his neck and without referring to any notes, he walked back and forth across the stage and spoke nonstop for two hours. He was spellbinding and I am sure every teacher there listened carefully to his every word. His topic: How to motivate your students to do well.

His message was very simple: show your students that you are genuinely interested in helping them to achieve academic success. Start by learning their names and call them by name at every opportunity so that you are recognizing each and every one of them as unique individuals. Show that you care passionately about the subject you are teaching. Your enthusiasm will be contagious. And he gave endless examples of students who greatly improved in their work at school because of the interest he showed in their welfare.

On another PD Day, I had the pleasure of meeting two teachers from Haliburton, Ontario, who came to Toronto to conduct a special workshop. I can't remember their names, but I will never forget what they told us. This was sometime in the 1980s, when every school was producing a mission statement to set forth its goals in education. At the school where I was teaching, the staff was divided into small groups to put these statements together. Then we assembled as a complete staff to report on what we had accomplished.

The result was a list of twelve goals we felt summed up what we were trying to accomplish as educators.

The two teachers from Haliburton and the staff at their school had gone through the same "mission statement" process and produced a list similar to the one we came up with at the school where I taught. But then what? All too often, the list gets filed away and forgotten. These two Haliburton teachers decided upon a different approach. They reduced their page-long list of mission statements to only three words:

RESPECT
COMMITMENT
RESPONSIBILITY

It was their belief that if they could impress these values upon their students, they would accomplish a great deal in their development, not only as students, but also as future citizens in our society.

A large sign bearing these three words was put on display in every classroom just above the clock because that is the part of the room which the students look at the most. From time to time, their teachers could pause in the middle of a lesson and discuss those words with their students — the meaning of each word and examples of each word in action.

I believed their idea had merit, and at the next staff meeting at our school, I proposed that we do the same in every one of our classrooms. The other teachers thought three words were insufficient for a mission statement, and a more detailed statement for our school had already been developed.

66

My First Call on a Cellphone

Heather Cirulis taught geography during the years that I taught history at North Toronto Collegiate. When I retired in June 1997, she read the following story aloud to all the teachers at our end-of-year luncheon:

> I remember Bill in the staff room at NT back in the early '80s when Jean Goodier was head of biology, when the secretaries used to try and find people whose calls came into the school for them, and when cellular phones were just coming into vogue.
>
> Jean was organizing a big conference that required her to be constantly available by phone and thus was carrying a cellular phone around with her. She entered the staff room with it one afternoon when I was in there with Bill and a few other people.
>
> Bill saw the cellular phone and, immediately deciding that he had to try this new invention, asked Jean if he might make a call.
>
> He dialled the school number. A secretary answered and Bill asked if he could please speak to Bill Sherk.
>
> A few moments later, one of the phones in the staff room rang. Bill answered that phone and said that yes, he would be happy to take a call and the secretary put Bill's call through to Bill who ended up having a conversation with himself on the phone while the rest of us watched the pantomime, figuring that we couldn't get better entertainment if we paid for it!
>
> Wishing you a long and happy retirement, Bill. And hoping that you can always find someone other than yourself to talk to.

67

My Farewell Address

Our end-of-year luncheon for North Toronto Collegiate teachers in June 1997 was held in the dining room of the Toronto Lawn Tennis Club near Summerhill and Yonge. After a delicious meal, my good friend and fellow history teacher John Laflair stood up and announced that I was about to deliver my farewell address before retiring from the teaching profession.

Before I had a chance to speak, he warmed up the crowd by leading them in a rousing rendition of one of my favourite songs: "Lloyd George Knew My Father, Father Knew Lloyd George."

This was sung to the tune of "Onward Christian Soldiers," which almost (but not quite) inspired the assembled crowd to march around the room while belting out the words. After the last note died down, it was my turn at the microphone.

In the first half of my address, I mentioned some of my fondest memories from thirty-one years of teaching, then spoke about what I was

John Laflair (left) and Bill Sherk at Bill's farewell luncheon in June 1997, leading the entire staff in a rousing, foot-stomping rendition of "Lloyd George Knew My Father" sung to the tune of "Onward Christian Soldiers."

planning to do with my new-found freedom. I told my fellow teachers that I would pursue a writing career focusing on the "autobiographies" of old cars by interviewing the owners of such vehicles and tracing their history from owner to owner. I was about to embark on a new career as a cross-Canada "carcheologist."

I told them a story I had often told to my students in grade ten Canadian History when we were studying the Great Depression. It was about a friend of mine named Ron Fawcett, an antique car restorer living at that time in Whitby, Ontario (Ron passed away in 2008 at age seventy-nine after restoring hundreds of vintage cars and supplying many of them for movies and television). I visited Ron on several occasions at his home to hear his stories. One day he told me about a 1922 Model T Ford Touring which had been in his family for over sixty years.

Ron was five years old when he and his parents were living in a rented house in Hamilton, Ontario. The year was 1934 during the Great Depression. Ron's dad had been out of work for weeks and had fallen behind with the rent. Their landlord told them they would be evicted from the house on Monday morning, along with their few pieces of furniture.

Then a miracle happened on Sunday evening. A man drove into their yard in an old Model T running on three cylinders and came to the back door. He told Ron's dad he had no money for gas to get home and was wondering if Ron's dad would buy the car from him for five dollars. Ron's dad said he was "financially embarrassed" and had no money at all.

The man said he could use a screen door. Could he have the screen door off the back of the house in exchange for the car? Ron's dad went to the kitchen, opened a drawer, took out a screwdriver, unscrewed the door, and handed the man the door, the screws, and the screwdriver. The man walked off down the street with the screen door under his arm, leaving behind his Model T Ford. The Fawcett family now had a getaway car.

Little Ron, only five years old, was sent up and down the street with a rubber hose and a gallon can to siphon some gas out of each of their neighbour's cars because the Model T was almost empty. His dad said, "If you hear a funny sucking sound from the bottom of their tank, put some gas back in because they're just about empty, too, and some of these people have to get to work the next day."

While Ron crept up and down the street after dark on his mission, his dad fixed the dead cylinder in the Model T and his mother gathered up all their belongings. They left town at midnight — just Mom and Dad and Ron and his dog — and drove all night until they reached some relatives on a farm near Drumbo, where they were allowed to stay for a short time.

The family had to keep moving in search of work and Ron attended fourteen schools while growing up. His dad painted some funny sayings all over the old Model T and drove it in parades for the next forty years to earn extra money. When he passed away in 1974, Ron took the steering wheel off the car and placed it in his dad's hands before closing the coffin.

With another steering wheel, Ron drove that old Model T for another thirty years in parades. Ron's son, Peter Fawcett, took over the car when Ron died and it's still in the same family, and it still runs.

Ron Fawcett restored hundreds of very expensive classic cars throughout his lifetime, but the car that meant the most to him was the Model T Ford — not only the one his family owned, but also the millions of other Model Ts built from 1908 to 1927 by Henry Ford.

I remember Ron saying to me: "He's the man who put the whole world on wheels. My only regret in life is that I never got to meet him and shake his hand."

I closed my farewell address with these words: "It has been an honour and a privilege for me to have been a teacher, and I want all of you to know that you have been like a second family to me, and North Toronto has been like a second home, and I hope our paths continue to cross many times in the years that lie ahead. I thank you."

Life After Teaching

Lady Catherine and Sir William.

68

"Are You Still Working on That Screenplay?"

Following my retirement from teaching in 1997, people often asked, "Well, Bill, now that you have all the time in the world, I guess you'll be finishing that screenplay you've talked about all these years."

My reply: "If only that were true. A very close friend of mine, Gord Hazlett, now ninety-two, tells me that life is like a roll of toilet paper. The closer we get to the end, the faster it goes!

"The screenplay has not been forgotten but has taken a new twist. The action still takes place on a single weekend in August 1957 in my home-town of Leamington, the Tomato Capital of Canada. And now that I'm living back here where I grew up, that might give me the edge I need to finish writing it."

I went on to explain that I am now writing it as a book, and if it becomes a bestseller, the movie can't be far behind.

These people then asked me, "Okay, that's fine, Bill, but how much of the book have you written yet?"

"I finally have the title and the first four sentences," I replied.

"That's all?"

"Yes, that's all. But it's a start."

The Coolest Nerd in Town

Seventeen-year-old Dean Armstrong slammed into the back of a parked car at thirty miles an hour. He was riding a bicycle. He somersaulted over the handlebars and landed in the driver's seat of a convertible, right beside a volup-tuous, blue-eyed blonde. The trouble that followed is still talked about today …"

"What happens next?" they want to know.
My reply: "I'm working on it!"

69

"David Letterman Calling!"

On Sunday, August 9, 1998, and just a year after my retirement from teaching high school, my 1947 Mercury convertible and I made a big splash in the *Toronto Star* in an article entitled "Retired History Teacher Tracks Down Cars." The subtitle read: "Teacher Now a 'Carchaeologist.'" It was written by a former student of mine, Lauren Blankstein:

> There were a few things a student could expect when they walked into Bill Sherk's history class: that he'd be wearing a pair of Levi's and bright white running shoes, and that they would be entertained.
>
> I know, because Mr. Sherk was my history teacher at North Toronto Collegiate Institute 10 years ago. He is referred to by many as Sherky, Sherk, Willy and plain old Bill, but to me, no matter the context, he will always be "Mr. Sherk."
>
> Words and the meanings that surround them take on a special significance for Mr. Sherk. His fascination with the English language and its Latin roots inspired him to write three books in which he coined new words.
>
> In the classroom he would share them with his students — "Farch" is the most memorable. Mr. Sherk asserted that melding the months of February and March into one would make the winter pass by faster. We would roll our eyes at his quirky ways, sometimes offering him a slight chuckle in the hopes of scoring extra marks.
>
> However, a decade later his idiosyncrasies no longer seem so strange. In fact it was his most recently coined term which led to our reunion. Mr. Sherk retired from

teaching last year and has delved into a new hobby. He's a "carchaeologist."

I explained to Lauren that a "carchaeologist" writes the auto-biography of individual cars. When you look at the cars coming down the assembly line, basically they're all the same because they're mass-produced. But once they leave the factory, every car becomes unique because every car goes to a different owner, and every car has its own unique story to tell from the showroom to the scrapyard. I love the challenge of tracking those stories down and writing about them.

Lauren continues:

> It all started when Mr. Sherk decided to try and find his very first car — a 1940 Mercury convertible. [I told her I memorized the serial number (1D5955) the day I bought the car (with no engine) on June 8, 1959.]
>
> It should be made clear that Mr. Sherk has the gift of an exceptional memory. He would start off each school year betting his students he could memorize their names overnight and each year he succeeded without fail. Mr. Sherk also has this uncanny ability to be able to tell anyone the actual day of the week they were born on if given the year and date of their birth …

I showed Lauren an old photo of me at seventeen standing beside my first car, which had no hubcaps. I told her that teenagers back then who owned their own cars took the hubcaps off and threw them away so that everyone would know it was their own car and not their father's car.

> During his teenage years he travelled between Leamington ("Tomato Capital of Canada, the car was tomato red," he proclaims), where his father was president of H.J. Heinz Company of Canada, and Toronto where he attended the University of Toronto Schools (UTS).

In 1959, he bought his '40 Merc and installed a 1957 Chevrolet 283 V8 engine. The car had its ups, but mostly it had its downs. He had to sit with his feet resting on the frame because there was no floor, he drove without exhaust pipes for a year (this served to ignite his date's front lawn when he thought he'd look cool and pull his car close to the front door and rev the engine), and at one point the hood flew off while driving.

Finally, he gave in and sold it in 1962.

The search for the 1940 Mercury began in 1988 — the year he taught me European history — and he found the car six years later in January 1994. Offering a reward of $150 (what he originally paid for the car in 1959), he placed ads in newspapers and made phone calls to as far away as Argentina.

I told Lauren I got a tip from someone who read a Toronto newspaper's review of my first book on old cars, *The Way We Drove: Toronto's Love Affair with the Automobile, 1893–1957*. That tip led me to Belleville and Laverne Allair who had been storing the 1940 Mercury, serial number 1D5955, in his garage and was planning to restore it when he retired.

"I was thrilled to know the car still exists. It looks beat up but it's solid and there's very little rust on the body," says Mr. Sherk, still clad as I remember him, in blue jeans and white running shoes. "I was really excited that after searching for six years and people telling me I was crazy to think it was still around, to actually discover the car and to be able to go and visit and to find all kinds of things on the car that reminded me of when I had it."

I told Lauren I checked the Ford Archives in Oakville and was told only 324 Mercurys like mine were built at the Ford plant in Windsor, Ontario.

Research also revealed that in its lifetime the Merc passed through the hands of 17 owners — eight owners prior to Mr. Sherk and eight after. The car was declared non-roadworthy by the OPP five years before he bought it, but shortly after, it was treated to a rebuild. In addition, he learned that since he sold the car it had only been on the road once and that was in 1966. At this point, a carchaeologist was born ...

On Friday, November 20, 1998, a call came in at North Toronto Collegiate from New York, inquiring about the article in the *Toronto Star*. The school phoned me with the name and number of the caller and I phoned New York and found myself talking to Bill Langworthy, saying he had read the article and was intrigued by the rediscovery of my first car.

"Are you saying," he wanted to know, "that you found a car like the one you owned as a teenager, or are you saying that you found the exact same car?"

"I found the very same car!" I proudly stated.

"That's amazing," he said. "I'm on the staff of the *David Letterman Show* and I am going to pass this along to the other staff people here. If we decide to have you on the show to talk about your car, we will give you a call."

I never heard from him again, but it was quite an honour to even be considered as a guest on the David Letterman Show. And all because I had bought an old car with no engine when I was seventeen and found the same car thirty-two years after I sold it!

In 2009, my long-lost 1940 Mercury convertible received an honourable mention in a story in the *Wall Street Journal!*

70

My Former Students Pop Up Everywhere

After I retired in June 1997, I occasionally encountered former students here and there around Toronto, and even in Leamington. Matt Zelsman was a student in my grade twelve Modern European History class. We saw each other on the platform of the Lawrence Avenue subway station one day. He was waiting for a southbound train and I was waiting for a northbound one.

He asked me if I was still writing for a newspaper called *Old Autos*. From time to time, I brought copies of that paper to class if some articles appeared that tied in with what we were studying. "Yes," I replied to Matt. "I've been writing for that paper since 1991."

He asked where he could get a copy of the current issue. We were standing beside a pay phone, so I dropped a quarter in and dialled 1-800-461-3457 to reach the office of the paper in Bothwell, Ontario. As soon as one of the office staff answered, I got my quarter back and said, "It's Bill Sherk calling. I'm putting one of my former students on the line. Please send him a complimentary copy of the current issue."

I handed the phone to Matt. He gave them his name and address, and they said the paper was on its way.

Just after he hung up, the southbound train rolled into the station. At the very same time, the northbound train also arrived. He stepped aboard his train, I stepped aboard mine, and we wished each other well as the doors closed and the two trains pulled out of the station.

A couple of years later, after watching a movie at the local theatre in my hometown of Leamington, some friends and I climbed into my tomato-red 1947 Mercury convertible, which was parked on the street close to the entrance to the show. Just before I turned the key to start the engine, a young woman on a bicycle stopped by the driver's window and said, "Mr. Sherk! What are you doing here?"

She had been a student of mine in grade ten Canadian History at North Toronto Collegiate about ten years earlier and saw the SHERK licence plate on my car. I told her I was now living back in my hometown following my retirement.

Then (wish I could remember her name) I asked her, "Now it's my turn to ask that same question. What are *you* doing here?"

She was in town for the summer, living on a farm and teaching English to the Mexican farm workers. At the end of the summer, she would be leaving for Japan to teach English over there.

Without my name on the licence plate, we might have missed one another.

71

Rocking Back and Forth

When I began teaching at Northern Secondary School, the head of the History Department was a kindly older gentleman named Graham Walker. He had a genuine love of history and did everything he could think of to instill that interest in his students, even to the point of playing "The Battle of New Orleans" by country singer Johnny Horton when teaching the War of 1812.

Years after I retired, I was in contact with Alan Nevins, who had Mr. Walker as a teacher. He reminded me that Mr. Walker had a habit of rocking back and forth on his feet when he was standing at the front of the room teaching a lesson. He was probably unaware that he was doing this.

One day, as Alan related the story to me, the class began rocking back and forth in time with Mr. Walker at the front of the room. He apparently did not notice this happening because the students were directly in front of him.

It was a large classroom with a pair of French doors in the centre of the north side of the room. These doors were the only entrance and exit for this room. Well, as Mr. Walker was rocking back and forth at the front of the room and as all his students were rocking back and forth at their desks in perfect time with their teacher, Vice-Principal Stewart Scott opened one of the doors and stepped into the room, apparently intending to speak to Mr. Walker about something.

The sight of the entire class rocking back and forth in perfect sync with the teacher at the front of the room was apparently something Mr. Scott had never seen before. He immediately did an about-face, stepped back out into the hall and closed the door quietly behind him, shaking his head in disbelief.

72

Cab Ride in Toronto

Chuck Reynolds from my hometown of Leamington, Ontario, where I now live, visited Toronto recently and rode in a cab. The driver asked Chuck where he was from, and he replied: "Leamington." The driver introduced himself as Perry Chan and said his history teacher at Northern Secondary School in Toronto in the late 1960s came from Leamington. His name was Mr. Sherk.

When I heard about this from Chuck, I suddenly remembered having Perry Chan in my Ancient and Medieval History class around 1968, when I was making use of a particular edition of a Donald Duck comic book to illustrate life in ancient Rome. The army was made up of small units of soldiers called maniples, and Perry one day handed me a sketch (now long gone) of "duckiples" in the Ro-Duck Army!

Perry, the next time I visit Toronto, I hope I can catch a ride in your cab.

73

I Pay Less Than $20 for Gas

After thirty-one years in the classroom, I had taught every history course on the high school curriculum from grade nine to grade thirteen and I was ready to try new things. I began writing newspaper articles and books about old cars all across Canada and the people who own them and drive them.

But I did not want to forget all the history I had taught for more than three decades. I had to devise a plan to keep all those historical dates fresh in my mind. "Use it or lose it!" I said to myself.

I decided to revisit all those dates in history whenever I stopped for gas. Unless we were on a trip somewhere and needed a full tank every time we stopped, I made a point of putting in less than twenty dollars' worth of gas. That way, the price on the pump matched a date in history. If I bought $17.89 worth, that would be 1789, the outbreak of the French Revolution. Or $18.67, the year of Confederation in Canada. Or $19.29, the year of the stock market crash. And of course one of the most famous dates of all time: 1492 for the year that Columbus sailed the ocean blue to the New World. That works out to only $14.92 for gas.

At our local 7-Eleven here in Leamington, a young man named Matt worked behind the counter, and he was a real history buff. He might have been a university student. Every time he saw me coming in, he looked at the amount on his screen ($19.12, for example) and said, "Well, Mr. Sherk, tell me the big news for that year!" Then we would talk about the sinking of the *Titanic*.

This arrangement worked well for all the years after the birth of Christ. But someone asked me one day how I would handle a date like 44 B.C., when Julius Caesar was assassinated. I said there's only one thing I could do. I would have to siphon 44 cents worth of gas out of my tank. And because I hate the taste of gasoline in my mouth (ever since I got a mouthful — see Chapter 12), I stay away from all the B.C. years.

In the photo you see here, I'm putting gas in my Enterprise rental car at the Esso station at Bayview and Broadway in Toronto after I retired from teaching. I pumped gas part-time at this station from January 1962 until the summer of 1963 while attending York University as a history student. See Chapter 12 for my adventures as a gas jockey.

74

Who's Afraid to Go to Mars?

In 2004, Dundurn asked me to write an updated version of *500 Years of New Words*, which, when first published, ended with the year 1983.

I had no problem finding a new word for every year from 1984 to 2003, but 2004 presented a problem. The book was scheduled for release in the spring of that year, which meant I only had the month of January to find a new word for that year. In desperation, and having been inspired by the latest news in the American space program, I invented one:

Marsiphobiphiliac (*MARZ-i-fo-bi-FEEL-ee-ak*): noun. A person who would love to go to Mars but is afraid of never returning home. (Greek: phobos — fear; philos — loving).

In January 2004, the United States landed two spacecraft on the surface of Mars: *Spirit* and *Opportunity*. Each one contained a rover designed to be driven across the surface to collect soil samples and conduct various experiments. The two spacecraft landed on opposite sides of the planet instead of side by side. If they were side by side, the two rovers might come out and smash into one another, making the United States responsible for the first car accident on another planet.

The updated version of *500 Years of New Words* came out in the spring of 2004. And maybe some of my former students are now training to become astronauts!

75

William Shakespeare or William Sherkspeare?

My knowledge of Shakespeare is limited to what I learned in high school and what I picked up while studying and teaching Elizabethan England (1558–1603). But my admiration for him is boundless. A few quotes have always stayed with me. The advice he gave to husbands to help them get along with their wives is brilliant:

"Be to her virtues very kind, and to her faults a little blind." The same advice could be given to wives to help them put up with their husbands.

My favourite all-time movie to show to my students was a thirty-minute motion picture entitled *The England of Elizabeth*, produced in colour by British Transport in 1957 and designed to encourage tourists to come to England.

William Shakespeare was born in 1564 and is first mentioned in the film when we see a wooden cradle on the floor at the foot of a four-poster bed. The narrator says: "Here is the cradle at Stratford-on-Avon. To John Shakespeare and Mary, his wife, a son. Now glance at the world of limitless wonder for a young mind to dream of, a fancy to range in. Cathay, newly mapped by the travellers and traders who followed Marco Polo ..."

The sonnet became a favourite style of poem for me when I had to memorize one in high school. Why did I like it so much? Because there was a space between the eighth and ninth lines, dividing it into two parts. If you could commit the first eight lines to memory, you were already over halfway there because you only had six more lines to go! "High Flight" (see page 133) was written over three hundred years after Shakespeare died, and yet it still uses the sonnet style that he employed so well.

If Shakespeare had been born in 1964 instead of 1564, he would have grown up during the horsepower race among the Big Three Detroit auto-makers. Surely he would have bought himself an old clunker as soon as he could scrape a few dollars together. And that car would become a subject for his writing. Now, and with apologies to William Shakespeare, I offer this pitiful poem (a work in progress) penned by William Sherkspeare:

Ode to My Old Car

Oh wretched pile of iron and steel,
With loathsome seats so vermin filled,
With four bald tires holding air,
And hubcaps gone to who knows where,
What hope have I to breathe new life
Into yon rusty hulk so foul,
Methinks it has no engine strong,
It really has no engine at all.

Hark! What newer engine do I see
In nearby wrecking yard for free!
With head held high and hopes on hold,
I drop it in yon gaping hole.
A turn of the key, a mighty roar,
And floorless, topless, we shall go!

76

Farewell, Jack Layton

Many years ago, Michael Layton was a student in my grade ten Canadian History class at North Toronto Collegiate. I can still see him sitting in the second desk in the row by the window. Many years later, on Saturday, August 27, 2011, I saw him again, this time on television. He was delivering a magnificent and heart-warming eulogy at the funeral service for his father, Jack Layton.

Someone once said that the greatest gift any human being can give to another is the gift of a good example, and I believe Jack Layton gave that gift to everyone he met. He believed passionately in social justice and worked tirelessly for the betterment of all Canadians, and especially for the most vulnerable members of our society.

I fondly remember chatting with Jack at Parents' Night about his son, Michael (a good student), and at the Broadview subway station, where he enjoyed greeting people and wishing them well. Once you met Jack, you felt you had gained a new friend.

I will never forget the letter he wrote to all Canadians two days before he died. It ended with these words:

"Love is better than anger. Hope is better than fear. Optimism is better than despair. So let us be loving, hopeful, and optimistic. And we'll change the world."

— Jack Layton 1950–2011

77

In Closing ...

My mother was right! This is the book I needed to write.

I stepped in front of my first class (and homeform) on Tuesday, September 6, 1966, a few minutes before 9:00 a.m., wondering if I would turn out to be a good teacher. The students themselves were a delight to teach, and I realized very quickly that I was exactly where I belonged.

This book has been, for me, a journey down memory lane spanning five decades of change and challenge and rewarding experiences. The students themselves made the journey all worthwhile, and I hope this book will bring back fond memories for them, as it has for me.

And the rewards? Here's one I will never forget. I had been teaching for about fifteen years when I received a postcard from two of my students — Kelly Macdonald and Valerie Sloan — who had taken my grade eleven Ancient and Medieval History course the previous year at North Toronto Collegiate. In the summer that followed, they travelled all through the Middle East and visited many of the places we had talked about in class. They ended the message on their postcard with these words: "Being here reminded us of you."

The Cars We Drove in High School

Whether you are a former student or teacher, think back to your high school days and the car or cars you were driving at that time, whether it was Dad's 1955 Oldsmobile 88 or the Model A roadster you hauled out of a junkyard.

For every story and photo published in Bill Sherk's syndicated newspaper column, you will receive a complimentary autographed copy of Bill Sherk's book, *Old Car Detective Favourite Stories, 1925 to 1965*.

To send your stories and photos, email *billtsherk@sympatico.ca* or write Bill Sherk, 25 John St., P. O. Box 255, Leamington, ON N8H 3W2.

Also by Bill Sherk

Old Car Detective
Favourite Stories, 1925 to 1965
978-1554889051
$19.99

In this hilarious collection of old car stories, Canada's very own "Old Car Detective" Bill Sherk presents eighty of his favourite stories from all ten provinces and spanning the years from 1925 to 1965. Behind every old car there's a story waiting to be told, all the way from your grandparents' Model T Ford to the Mustang you drove in high school. All the stories and photographs in this book are in chronological order from 1925 to 1965, giving you a forty-year journey through Canada's rich automotive heritage and brought to life by the people who owned and drove the cars of yesteryear — and some still do!

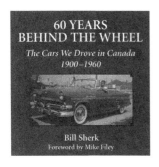

60 Years Behind the Wheel
The Cars We Drove in Canada, 1900–1960
978-1550024654
$24.99

From rumble seats and running boards to power tops and tailfins, *60 Years Behind the Wheel* captures the thrill of motoring in Canada from the dawn of the twentieth century to 1960. There are intriguing stories of cars with no steering wheels, and fascinating photographs of historic vehicles from across the country. From the Studebaker to the Lincoln-Zephyr, from the showroom to the scrapyard, here are over 150 vehicles owned and driven by Canadians.

500 Years of New Words

The Fascinating Story of How, Why, and When Hundreds of Your Favourite Words First Entered the English Language
978-1550025255
$24.99

500 Years of New Words takes you on an exciting journey through the English language from the days before Shakespeare to the first decade of the twenty-first century. All the main entries are arranged not alphabetically, but in chronological order, based on the earliest known year that each word was printed or written down. This book can be opened at any page and the reader will discover a dazzling array of linguistic delights.

I'll Never Forget My First Car

Stories from Behind the Wheel
978-1550025507
$24.99

In this hilarious collection of stories, *Old Autos* columnist Bill Sherk describes in vivid detail the trials and tribulations of those brave souls who, throwing caution to the wind and money down the drain, made the fateful decision that would forever change the course of their lives. They went out and bought their very first cars. And whether it came from the showroom or the scrapyard, your first car was your ticket of admission into the adult world. Gas, oil, repairs, tow trucks, speeding tickets, insurance, and fender benders would take a vacuum cleaner to your bank account, but you didn't care. You were behind the wheel and on the road.

Available at your favourite bookseller.

www.dundurn.com

What did you think of this book?
Visit www.dundurn.com for reviews, videos, updates, and more!